To Judith, who encouraged

Glimpses of Biblical Women And Other Poems

By Dorothy J. Mosher

Illustrated by David Mosher

Westview
Publishing Inc.

part thereof in any form whether in print, electronic format or any other media. Reviewers may use brief excepts with permission of the author or publisher.

Printed on alkaline paper

First Edition

Printed in the United States of America

ISBN 0-9755646-1-7

Other prepress work by Westview Publishing, Inc.
Hugh Daniel, Acquisitions Editor
Paula Underwood Winters, cover design and layout

Westview
Publishing, Inc.
8120 Sawyer Brown Road, Suite 107
Nashville, Tennessee 37221
(615) 646-6131
http://www.westviewpublishing.com

Acknowledgements

This book has been a long time in composition. I was fortunate to work for the Division of Educational Ministries at the National Council of Churches during the creation of two important events. The emphasis on inclusive language began in the 1970's with the publication of An Inclusive Language Lectionary Years A-C. The edition of the New Revised Standard Version Bible was published in 1989. Both of these events led me to think more deeply about women in the Bible.

Those thoughts eventually led to this collection.

I am grateful to Pat Floyd, who read my first nine poems and encouraged me to write more.

Thanks to Diane Luton Blum who wrote the introduction and never stopped believing in me.

Gratitude to Martha Whitemore Hickman, who wrote the preface.

To my husband, Bruce, many thanks for your computer expertise.

To Dave, my oldest son, who readily volunteered some of his Christmas vacation time to illustrate the poems.

- To *The Women's Bible Commentary* by Carol A. Newsom and Sharon H. Ringe, editors for setting me on a path of learning more about women in the Bible. This book gave me a context for writing these poems.

I acknowledge the following poems:

Bread, 1996 and May My First Waking Thought,1997, *The Prayer Calendar,* General Board of Global Ministries, The United Methodist Church. Used with permission.

Invitation (Epiphany 1997) and Illumined, (Pentecost 1997). *Sacramental Life.* Used with permission.

First Lent, March 1995, *Relay,* Greater New Jersey Annual Conference. Used with permission.

Scripture quotes are from the New Revised Standard Version of the Bible, ©1989 by the National Council of Churches of Christ in the USA. Used by permission. All rights reserved.

Scripture quotations designated TEV are from the Good News Bible, The Bible in Today's English Version - Old Testament, ©American Bible Society 1976.

Introduction

by the Rev. Diane Luton Blum

In the patriarchal world of the Old and New Testament communities of faith we find a great variety of divine and human expectations for women. Sometimes the prevailing cultural view of the place of women has been adopted by the faith community, as in the case with Samuel's mother, Hannah and in the household of King David with his plural wives. Sometimes the cultural expectations are transcended by the roles permitted women in the faith community, for example, Deborah is a judge and a military leader, and when Mary and Elizabeth take center stage in relation to their husbands supporting roles. Sometimes the faith community is the origin for a narrow role for women that is religiously enforced, as in the case of the Levirate marriage rules which impact and shape the lives of Tamar, Naomi and Ruth.

The poetry of Dorothy J. Mosher opens up these worlds for her readers in all their splendid diversity and humanity. By focusing primarily on women whose stories are barely glimpsed, we are invited by each poem to use our senses and intuition to read and live between the lines of these amazingly plentiful stories. One story poem leads to another. Mosher's insight and scholarship encourage her readers to open the Bible for more. Using the poetic form, this collection bears evidence of thorough exegesis and biblical study. We as readers stand to learn more about the Christian scriptures and the human worlds through which they have come.

One of Mosher's many gifts to her readers is the clear, dynamic portrait of the way in which each woman copes with her unique circumstances. By selecting both the heroic, like Mary, and the expedient, like Herodias, the simple, like the unnamed widow who loved Tabitha, and the cunning, like Tamar, the educated, like Huldah, and the outsider, like Orpah, the proud, like Sapphira, and the humble, like Hannah, Mosher introduces for us a broad selection of coping skills, choices and faith among all these women. We are invited to recognize ourselves and one another in these poems of often forgotten women. We are invited by the questions that follow each poem to journal, or to share in group study to "Think about these things," rehearsing our own future choices. Readers are led to prayerfully rehearse a divine summons in our own circumstances to enter the roles of peacemakers, benefactors, prophets and friends.

SUGGESTIONS FOR USE

This collection is readily available to the reader who is searching for a study aid, both alone and with a group or class. The book lends itself to individual meditation and devotional use, encouraging the reader to journal in response to the section, "Think about these things." Groups using this resource can focus on spiritual formation experiences by praying together, reflecting on the questions and committing support one's fellow participants for faithful actions that flow from new insights.

The poems are well suited to reading aloud in order to savor the many voices that Mosher brings to life. The music of the free verse many inspire the reader to use verse in journaling as she/he responds to "Think about these things." Whether the reader is alone or in a group, this poetry is meant for the voice as well as the mind, for the heart as well as the intellect.

Established Bible Study Groups and Classes will find this resource to be a refreshing way to approach scripture from the "margins" typically occupied by so many of these women. Whether the group is all women or mixed men and women, participants are invited to use these poems to look back to the persons we have often believed to be the "main characters," like Peter and Paul, Samuel and David, Moses and John the Baptist. Each introduction provides stimulating scholarship and the sections for "Think about these things," may be used to activate sharing, discussion, prayer and plans for action. Leaders or teachers can bring additional resources now available about women in the Bible to expand this study, allowing each poem to provide a weekly focus. Leaders and teachers should encourage participants to consider the many applications of these poems to our contemporary lives of discipleship, family decisions and community transformation.

For women's groups, fellowship or prayer groups, these poems can provide an excellent basis for programs. Again, poetry is meant to be heard and enacted, not just read. The reader or leader is invited to consider pairing favorite hymns and songs that carry themes from the lives of these biblical women into our lives of celebration and praise, lament and hope. Group participants might be encouraged to find specific psalms which give expression to the faith and circumstances of each woman glimpsed through Mosher's poems, then pairing them with contemporary music familiar to the group.

Readers may consider using the poems as a worship resource. The reader and listener alike can be transported by the distinctive voices of each biblical woman, moving more deeply into the biblical messages chosen for worship celebrations and seasonal observances. The poems can be used in preaching, or in dramatization, with appropriate costume and staging. Mosher delivers poignant closing lines that deliver a powerful, thought-provoking impact.

Some or all of these poems could be used to shape a biblically based retreat. Depending on the time available, number of participants, this collection could allow for lively reenactments, and active discussion sessions based on "Think about these things." Individual time alone with the poems, journaling and perhaps writing more prayers and verse, can be balanced by larger group activities, the formulation of plans for application and living commitments to new acts of faith.

I give thanks to God for this faithful detective who has looked through the keyholes of research and imagination to glimpse women we readers can now know in unforgettable ways. I am grateful for Mosher's listening ear and compassionate heart which grant us moving images and music of God's beloved daughters living so long ago. I hope in your reading and reflecting your own eyes of faith will be opened to glimpse the mothers, sisters, enemies, friends, rulers, and servants that God brings into our paths. May we greet each other, like Mary and Elizabeth, with recognition, joy and God's shalom.

Table of Contents

HEBREW SCRIPTURES:

1. Hagar   Genesis 21-1-21 3

2. Mrs. Lot Genesis 19 7

3. Tamar   Genesis 38... 10

4. Milcah   Numbers 27:1-11; 36:5-12 14

5. Rahab   Joshua 2 19

6. Achsah   Judges 1:11-15 24

7. Orpah   Ruth 1 28

8. Hannah   1 Samuel 1:1-20 33

9. Abigail   1 Samuel 26 38

10. Huldah   2 Kings 22; 2 Chronicles 34 43

NEW TESTAMENT

11. Mary and Elizabeth   Luke 1:9-56 48

12. Elizabeth   Luke 1 51

13. Mary and the Wise Men   Matthew 2:1-12 55

14. Anna   Luke 2:36-38 58

15. Woman with a Hemorrhage   Mark 5:25-4 61

16. Herodias   Mark 6:17-29 65

17. Woman taken in adultery   John 8:1-11 69

18. Procula   Matthew 27:19 72

19. Sapphira   Acts 5:1-11 76

20. A Widow of Joppa   Acts 9:36-43 80

21. Rhoda   Acts 12:12-17 84

Other Poems

Preface to Other Poems	89
May My First Waking Thought	90
Evening Prayer	92
Bread	93
All of Your Life Is One with God	94
First Lent	96
Getting Through the Days	97
Invitation	98
The Creche in the Kitchen	100
Leaf Time in Pennsylvania	!01
Crossroads	102
Prayer While Making Communion Bread	104
An English Idyll	106
Pantry	108
Celtic Prayer for a Garden	110
Daily Obligation	112
April's Brief Affair with Winter	113
Illumined	114
Smooring the Fire	116
I Will Write My Poems	117
Ever Widening Circles	118
Quiet Time	120
Advice for Christians	121
Thoughts from Study of 1 John	122
A Sense of Place	123
Snorkelers Need Not Apply	124
The Retirement Window	125
Relationships	126
Thanks Times Five	127

Hebrew Scriptures

A Glimpse of.... Hagar

Hagar, an Egyptian slave, served Sarah, Abraham's wife. Sarah had never had children, and was growing old, so she offered Hagar to Abraham. In the ancient world, since children were so needed to continue the tribe's existence, surrogate motherhood was accepted. Abraham went into Hagar's tent, and she conceived. She called the child, Ishmael.

After the birth Sarah felt threatened by Hagar's position, even though she was a slave. The entire story is told in Genesis 16-18:15.

This glimpse of Hagar is concerned with the last part of the story: Sarah's resentment of Hagar and her child; Sarah's driving them out of the camp; and of Abraham's providing food and water for their journey.

Being a slave, Hagar had few options to change her situation. Perhaps she erred when she displayed her motherhood too openly in front of Sarah. In many ways, Hagar does not use her wits to save herself.

Yet, in spite of all these miscalculations she is still listed in the Bible as the first woman to talk with God personally. Hagar and her son escaped the desert and flourished. She is known as the mother of the Arab nations.

PRAYER: Oh God, help us not to be victims of circumstance. May we be strong leaders who help others. Amen.

Hagar

Genesis 21:1-21

Oh, my brown-skinned beauty, my Ishmael!.
You stay far behind me dragging your feet.
I cannot blame you, but we must stay together.

The sun's so hot. Our water's disappearing.
I hate to think of what will happen
when the water's gone.

This morning, when the dew lay on the grasses
Ishmael's father, known as Abraham,
came to me with bread, a skin of water
and sent us away from the camp.

Sarah made him do it!
She hates me. Ishmael is Abraham's first son,
conceived with Sarah's blessing - she was barren.
She was old and far beyond the way of women.
I thought I had the upper hand with Abraham,
for how can an old crone bring forth a child?
But I was wrong, and now pay the price.

Who would have guessed when those three men came by
Predicting Sarah's womb filled with a baby
that it would come to pass.
Sarah didn't believe it, for she giggled
and then denied it when Abraham confronted her.

But when Sarah's body filled with growing child,
she laughed a hearty laugh. It chilled my bones.
Since I was but a slave her son would be first
in Abraham's eyes, though my son was born first.
Even so, I hoped Ishamael would receive a blessing.

Yesterday the camp celebrated.
In honor of the weaning of Isaac,
Abraham gave a feast for all the company.
The day went well, the wine flowed freely,
the lamb well cooked, figs and grapes to eat.

Glimpses of Biblical Women & Other Poems

Ishmael was playing with the baby
when a screech from Sarah stilled the multitude.
She stood in front of Abraham and shouted
   "Cast out this slave woman with her son;
     for the son of this slave woman shall not inherit
     along with my son, Isaac."

Ishmael and I fled to our tent
and there we stayed
until Abraham sent us on our way this morning.

Come here, boy, sit under this bush.
It may protect you from that raging sun.
A drink of water?
There is little left, but you may have it.
Now close your eyes and rest while you can.

Abraham was sorry we were leaving.
He gave us bread and water for our trip.
But he must know about the desert's perils.
He sent us to our doom, though he'd deny it.

Now the boy's eyes flicker and his body
slumps with the hand of sleep upon him.
I must move away, I cannot watch
my son dying here before my eyes.
I love him so, and now...my tears mourn him.
May his end be soon, if he must die.

Then as I weep, I hear a voice from heaven
   "What troubles you, Hagar?
   Do not be afraid;
   for God has heard the voice of the boy
     where he is.
   Come lift up the boy and hold him fast
     with your hand,
   for I will make a great nation of him."

My eyes pop open when I hear the voice.
There before me stands a well of water.
So I fill the skin and hurry to my Ishamel
who drinks the water with great swallows
wipes him mouth with his hand
looks at me, and laughs.

"Finally, beloved, whatever is true, whatever is honorable whatever is just, whatever is pure, whatever is pleasing, whatever is commendable, if there is anything worthy of praise. (Philippians 4:8) NRSV

Think about these things...
Hagar

In a time when women's status was enhanced with childbirth, Hagar must have felt she had the upper hand. Sarah's pregnancy changed that. Hagar's expulsion from the community placed her in a difficult position. In spite of her troubles. She was the first woman to talk to God face to face.

How do you deal with adversity? Does it overwhelm you? Can you see your way through it? Is your faith a help in that situation?

A Glimpse of... Mrs. Lot

Mrs. Lot—we don't even know her name—is on the way to a new home, as her old home burns to the ground. She is a self-centered person, more concerned about her appearance and comfort than about the cataclysm taking place in Sodom. From a comfortable lifestyle she has been reduced to the status of refugee.

She is swept up in a happening with little explanation from others, and fails to see the urgency with which she must move. Since she falls behind the rest of her family and travels alone and unobserved, she believes she can look back and see her home. Her logic is one many use: "Who would know?"

It's easy to criticize Mrs. Lot. She shouldn't have looked back. Yet, when cataclysms come in our lives, isn't that what we do? We look back, trying to figure out what went wrong, what we could have done differently. We fight change because it is scary and sometimes deny the reality of the present.

Mrs. Lot represents for me the human dilemma with which we all live. Some of us deal with it better than others, but all of us, in treasuring our memories, look back. May Mrs. Lot be a reminder to us to look forward also.

PRAYER: O God, help us treasure the essence of our memories. May they empower us for the journey ahead, not enmesh us in the past. Amen.

Mrs. Cot

Genesis 19:1-26

Lot called me from my bed:
"Quick! Quick! Collect your things,
We have to go."

I didn't know
nor did he tell me,
why we had to leave in such a hurry.

I'm sure those travellers who came yesterday
had something to do with this.

I hardly slept at all
what with those shouting townsmen
and their filthy propositions.

We saved those stranger's lives!
And how are we repaid?
This morning, half asleep, a quarter dressed,
one of them grabbed me by the arm most sharply,
pushing me ahead of him out of the door.
"Run!" he said, "and don't look back."
(I could not gather paint and perfumes)

If only I could sit a minute.
My feet pain me so, my heart pains more.
Yet Lot is unaware of me.
He and the girls move on.

...Just one last look
Who would know?

If only I could see the street once more
and through the courtyard see our house.
My life is there and only there.
Oh—all gone now—flames and ashes everywhere!

How strange, I cannot move my feet!
The salt upon my lips—I....

Think about these things...
Mrs. Lot

How often do you resist change, even though you know that change is a constant? What are some innovations you could try practicing to help ease the pain of change and help you look forward to another situation?

Change is very hard for me sometimes. After reading today's lesson I need to go to the Lord more in prayer when I become upset about a change.

Zoar (means small)

A Glimpse of...Tamar

The story of Tamar is not one you are likely to hear read in the Sunday worship service at church. This story is filled with deception and illicit sexuality. She is a woman who used her wits in an unbearable situation. Look for her name in the geneology of Jesus in Matthew, chapter one.

Tamar is married twice to sons of Judah. The first marriage does not produce an heir. Her husband dies and she is married shortly to her brother in law. The Levirate law under which Jewish family life was governed, commanded a brother to take the widow of a deceased brother who died childless and, with her, beget a son to continue his brother's line. The second brother did not wish to do that, and was summarily punished for his insolence. There is another brother but he is too young. So Tamar is sent home to her family with no position in society.

Tamar throughout this story tries to fit in and find her place. But obviously, the Levirate Law is not being fulfilled, because neither her brother-in law nor her father-in-law will fulfill their responsibilities to her. Tamar finds herself dispossessed through no fault of her own. But being a resourceful woman, she resorts to trickery to regain her position.

PRAYER: Mother God: help us be strong and resourceful enough to find our places in your plan. Amen.

Tamar
Genesis 38

Where is my place? I have no place!
Twice widowed by the sons of Judah!
People say they were evil men.
I do not think they deserved to die.

Er did evil in the sight of God
and was punished with death.
Then Er's brother, Onan, married me on Judah's order,
his duty in the Levirate law.
But Onan spilled his seed upon the ground
rather than impregnate me
and I despised him for it!. That is the law.
The first born son would be deemed Er's child.
When Onan died, I saw his death
as punishment from the Lord.

So I lost twice. I was a good wife,
but that made no difference.
With neither child nor husband,
I was no longer a virgin
nor was I a widow with young issue.
Judah, my father-in-law, sent me
back to my father's house to wait for Shelah
Er's young brother, not yet a man..

I waited for the younger brother, Shelah,
to grow to manhood, so we could be married.
Judah has promised this to me.
But he showed signs of mistrust,
as if I'd caused the deaths of his two sons.
I am no sorceress!

So I existed in my father's house
with no place of my own.
I was looked down upon, despised, a failure
seething at my humiliation.

When Judah's wife died, I saw a chance
to right the wrong and give Er a child.
I wrapped myself in temple garb
and stationed myself along the path

A Glimpse of Biblical Women & Other Poems

Judah would walk on his way to Timnah.
His eyes lit up when he saw me
but he did not recognize me.
He was eager for my services
—offered to send a goat as payment—
but I demanded his seal with its cord
and his walking stick
as pledge until the goat was sent.
He yielded them quickly and
breathing heavily, he knew me.

Judah's friend could not find the temple harlot
when he brought the goat as payment for the pledge.
I went back home and waited hoping finally
my womb would bear a child.
Hardly three months passed when gossip came
to Judah's ears that I was pregnant.

"Will I never be rid of that woman?" he bellowed
"She has been playing whore;
she must be burned. She's Shelah's betrothed
and guilty of adultery."

But when the day for judgment came for me
I showed no fear. I pulled the seal and cord
and walking stick from my garments
and held them out for all the crowd to see.
"The man who made me pregnant owns to these,"
I said and looked at Judah. Murmurs ceased.

Judah's bellicosity collapsed, he blushed,
he shook his head, as if to clear his mind,
then sadly nodded his assent.
"Tamar is more righteous than I am,
She was rejected, and the fault is mine.
Come, Tamar, to your rightful home once more."
And so I went.

As if to make up for the years of pain
I birthed two fine twin boys.
The delivery was strange, however..
One baby poked his hand out, and the midwife,
eager to name the first born child,
tied a red string around the hand.

But the child pulled his hand back in my womb,
and the other child was born first!
They were named Perez and Zerah,
sons of Judah. Now I can rest secure.

Think about these things...
Tamar

Desperate people do desperate things. In spite of her humiliation, Tamar took a wild chance, endangering her body and her reputation.

Have you ever felt blocked by someone else's actions? What did you do? What was the outcome?

A Glimpse of... Milcah
One of the daughters of Zelophehad

This story about five daughter of Zelophohad of the tribe of Manasseh is unique in the Bible. The crux of the story pertains to inheritance of the land. Years before Moses had consulted the Lord about giving land to the women - namely the daughters of Zelaphohad. Moses received an affirmative answer from the Lord. At that time, however, the tribes of Israel were still wandering in the wilderness.

The tribes moved into Moab, just across the Jordan from the Promised Land. Moses ordered a census as a way of sorting our the members of the different tribes. The daughters came to Moses once again with their request. In the meantime, the men of the tribe of Manasseh showed great concern because if the daughters inherited the land and married outside the tribe, that land would be lost. Therefore, as a stipulation for receiving the inheritance, Moses commands the women to marry within their tribe. Usually daughters married out of their tribes to avoid genetic diseases among any offspring.

The daughters were concerned about keeping their father's name alive in the tribe, but the men who feared loss of tribal property switched the emphasis toward owning the land. When the daughters married, the land would go to their husbands anyway. The men of the tribe of Manasseh made sure that their husbands belonged to the same tribe as the daughters.

What courage it must have taken for the women to bring the inheritance case before Moses. Their names are: Mahlah (gentleness), Noah (flattery), Hoglah (magpie), Milcah (counsel) and Tirzah (delight).

PRAYER: In our relationships with men, O God, we may often be at a disadvantage. Keep before us the example of the daughters of Zelophohad, so we may be strong, as well as caring. Amen.

Milcah

Numbers 27:1-11; 36: 5-12

My name is Milcah.
I am one of the five daughters of Zelophohad
of the tribe of Manassah.

Our father died in the wilderness
leaving no son, just five daughters.
We had not crossed the Jordan yet to take the land
but already the tribal men were busy
trying to secure the best sites possible.

We five held counsel among ourselves.
We could see what was happening.
The land would be apportioned to the men
We would have nothing—no land to celebrate
our father's name.
Drastic action was called for.

I was chosen to speak for our rights.
It was not easy requesting audience with Moses
He spoke to God as I am speaking to you.
No one else in all Israel had done that.
Yet, we believed we had a claim
and unless we pursued it
we would be landless, and our father, only a memory.

Moses commissioned a census on the plain.
All the tribes with people over twenty years
came to be counted.
Our tribe of Manasseh came last, Manasseh being
one of Joseph's sons.

We stood before Moses who sat with Eliezer the priest,
and all the leaders in the tent of meeting.
We five stood together for support
but I stepped forward to present our case.

> "Our father died in the wilderness," I said.
> "He was not among the company of those
> who gathered themselves together against the Lord

in the camp of Kohrah, but died in his own sin;
and he had no sons.
Why should the name of our father be taken away
from his clan because he had no son?
Give to us a possession among our father's brothers."

Moses seemed uncertain what to say to us.
Such a case as this had never come before him.
He begged time to present our case to the Lord.
We nodded and stepped back.

Later Moses spoke to us the words the Lord had told him.
"The daughters of Zelophohad are right in what they are
saying;
You shall indeed let them possess an inheritance
among their father's brothers
and pass the inheritance of their father on to them.
You shall also say to the Israelites,
If a man dies, and had no son, then you shall pass
his inheritance on to his daughter.
If he has no daughter, then you shall give his
inhertance to his brothers.
If he has no brothers then you shall give his
inheritance to his father's brothers.
and if his father has no brothers, then you shall give
his inheritance to the nearest kinsman of his clan,
and he shall possess it.'"

We were delighted with the Lord's words,
but several of our kinsmen grumbled loudly.
They saw no reason for us to inherit.
We would marry and the land would be divided
and given to the husbands we had chosen.
The land the tribe sought for itself,
would go to another tribe, not to Manasseh.
When the time of Jubilee arrived
and land must be returned to former owners,
that land would be added to those tribes
we'd married into and would be lost forever to Manasseh.

Moses saw the truth in their complaining
So, turning to the men who grumbled, he said
"Let them marry whom they think best;
only it must be into a clan of their father's tribe

that they are married, so that no inheritance
of the Israelites shall be transferred
from one tribe to another;
for all Israelites shall retain the inheritance
of their ancestral tribes. Every daughter
who possesses an inheritance in any tribe
of the Israelites shall marry one from the clan
of her father's tribe, so that all Israelites
may continue to possess their ancestral heritage.
No inheritance shall be transferred from one tribe
to another; for each of the tribes of the Israelites
shall retain its own inheritance."

We agreed to the terms. We'd won far more
than we had ever dreamed,
and if it meant marrying our cousins, to fulfill the Lord's
command, we were happy to do it.

So, we married our cousins.
Five weddings on a single day
fulfilled our obligations to the tribe
and our beloved father.

I'd be inclined to wager that within a year or two
one of the babies from these unions
will be called Zelephohad.

Think about these things...
Milcah

As late as the nineteenth century in the United States, women could not own property or vote. It took years and untold effort on the part of suffragettes to open opportunities for women.

The church also remained male dominant until recent times. What does this story of five women fighting partriachial religious leaders say to you about your role in the church or community life of today? Does it give you courage to persevere?

A Glimpse of... Rahab the Harlot

Prostitutes have a special place in the Biblical world. The fertility cults of Caanan flourished, associated closely with the farming activities of the people. But Rahab is not a temple prostitute.

The two spies evidently believe that they can hide from public view better in a prostitute's house. The neighborhood is used to seeing strange men coming and going to Rahab's house.

Rahab recognizes the truth in the worship of Yahweh. She exhibits courage in hiding the spies and lying to the king's guards. Her loyalty lies with her family and their welfare.

Rahab is mentioned in scripture as a woman of faith, in spite of her occupation. (See Hebrews 11:31 and James 2:25). Matthew includes her in his geneology of Jesus, because she became the wife of Salmon, who was Boaz's father and Ruth's father-in-law. A woman of faith and loyal to family; adaptable to new situations and clever enough to take advantage of them. This is Rahab.

PRAYER: God, you see behind the facade we show to the world. You know us completely. Give us courage to make the right decisions. Give us imagination to conceive greater things in your name. Amen.

Rahab the Harlot

Joshua 2

The two men came to my house at noon.
I thought they might be spies,
but I don't ask questions,
I'm here to serve.

Jericho teemed with excitement;
rumors were rife that the Israelite army
camped at Shittim would soon invade our city.
Most citizens placed faith in our strong walls,
but I remembered how the Israelite army
destroyed much larger forces than our own,
and we lay directly in their path!

The two men would be found if the king's men came
- and they assuredly would come,
so I took the spies to the rooftop where
I ret the flax to make the linen clothes.
They lay down on the roof upon the stalks
I covered them with other stalks till they were hid.

The pounding on my door revealed the king's men
sent to find the spies. I bade them enter.
"Bring out the men who have come to you,"
"who entered your house," one said,
"for they have come to search out the whole land."

"True," I replied, "the men came to me
but I did not know where they came from.
And when it was time to close the gate at dark,
the men went out. Where the men went I do not know.
Pursue them quickly, for you can overtake them."

The soldiers searched my house
even the roof - though not for very long.
The powerful stink of flax did its work
They left me soon with puzzled expressions.
I was relieved when the search was done,
and after careful waiting to be sure
no king's spy lingered,
I scurried to the roof, and we connived together.

Glimpses of Biblical Women & Other Poems

"I know the Lord has given you the land," I said,
and that dread of you has fallen upon us,
and that all the inhabitants of the land
melt in fear before you.
For we have heard how the Lord dried up
the water of the Red Sea before you
when you came out of Egypt,
and what you did to the two kings of the Amorites
that were beyond the Jordan, to Sihom
and Og, whom you utterly destroyed.
As soon as we heard it, our hearts melted,
and there was no courage left in any of us
because of you. The Lord your God
is indeed God in heaven above and on earth below.

Now then, since I have dealt kindly with you,
swear to me by the Lord that you in turn
will deal kindly with my family.
Give me a sign of good faith that you will spare
my father and mother, my brothers and sisters,
and all who belong to them, and deliver our lives from
death.'

"Our life for yours!," they said.
"If you do not tell this business of ours,
then we will deal kindly and faithfully
with you when the Lord gives us the land."

I made ready to lower them by a rope
over the city wall.

"Go toward the hill country," I said,
"so that the pursuers may not come upon you.
Hide yourselves there three days,
until the pursuers have returned;
then afterward you may go your way."

The bargain was struck, but they lingered still.
"We will be released from this oath
you have made us swear to you
if we invade the land and you do not tie
this crimson cord in the window
through which you let us down,
and you do not gather into your house

your father and mother,
your brothers and all your family.
If any of you go out of the doors
of your house into the street,
they shall be responsible for their own death,
and we shall be innocent;
but if a hand is laid upon any
who are with you in the house,
we shall bear the responsibility for their death.
But if you tell this business of ours,
then we shall be released from this oath
that you made us swear to you."

"I said to them,"According to your word,
so be it."
The rope in place, they plunged in darkness then,
one after the other.
I held my breath that no one's wakefulness
detected them rappelling in the night.

There is nothing to do now but take my duties up once more:
to make the beds and wash the dishes clean,
and wait...wait for the armies of their God.

Now as I stand looking over the wall
I wonder if the spies will be reminded
of their solemn pledge to spare my brood.

Well, it's too late now.
Nor would I change my bargain.
The scarlet cord flutters from the window post.
I've cast my lot with Israel's strong God
and I can do no more.

Think about these things...
Rahab

Hiding spies is risky business. Think of others who took the challenge: people who hid slaves during the Underground Railway days; Corrie Ten Boom hiding Jews in her house; Eric Schindler hiding Jews in his factory. In the 70's church people activated the Sanctuary rule, hiding refugees from Central America from the Border Patrols.

What did all these people have in common?

A Glimpse of...Achsah

This story comes from the book of Joshua with a repeat in Judges.

Caleb, a member of the tribe of Judah, is a military commander, charged with winning an area of the Promised Land. Caleb's land lies in the vicinity of Hebron, but he wishes to extend his holdings.

As a prize of war he offers his daughter, Achsah, to the man who takes the town of Keriath-Sepher, which is also called Debir. Othniel, a young handsome soldier, rises to the challenge and captures the town for the Hebrews. Then he comes to claim his prize, the lovely Achsah. Othniel's victory serves as payment for the bride.

Achsah, seeing that the land is being divided among family members, asks Caleb for some land. He gives the couple land in the Negeb.

But Achsah and Othniel discover that the land they have been given is desert land. Achsah returns to Caleb with her request for springs. Caleb grants her wish.

Othniel became the first major judge chronicled in the book of Judges.

PRAYER; Give us us patience, Oh God, to keep asking for the things we need. Keep us thankful for the things we have, and help us always to be willing to share with others. Amen.

Achsah

Joshua 15:13-19; Judges 1:11-15

I first saw Othniel at Hebron
after my father, Caleb, took the city in the Lord's name.
My father, is a mighty warrior.
During the wilderness sojourn he was sent with a group
of men as spies to see the lay of the land in Caanan
before the Israelites took it.
When they returned Moses got two stories.

My father told him that indeed the land was
  blessed with milk and honey.
Caleb and Joshua had picked a clump of grapes as proof.

But the other men
tried to disprove Caleb and Joshua's story.
We did not try to take the land then
just because the people became fearful
and did not trust the Lord to help them.

Now, years later, we have crossed the Jordan.
My father, Caleb, moved into Caanan
and is quartered at Hebron.
But there was more conquest to be done.
My father asked his troops to take Keriath Sepher
—a town near here.
"I will give my daughter, Achsah, in marriage
to the man who attacks and captures Keriath Sepher.

Othniel, my uncle's son, took the challenge.
He was a handsome young man and a good soldier.
I watched him march his men that day.
My heart leaped within me to see him go.
I hoped they would be successful in their raid.

One morning I awoke to shouts of town's people.
They were praising Othniel, who had captured Keriath-Sepher.
Then I knew my fate was linked with his.

My father gave us a wedding present of land
    that lay in the Negeb.
This land was ours at last.
The land our people had dreamed
and longed for during those forty years.

Othniel and I went to look at our land.
We were disappointed.
The field was arid desert.
How were we to make it bloom?

"We must have springs if we can farm this land,"
I said to Othniel. "I will ask my father."

We returned to Caleb, bowed to the the ground,
and thanked him for his gift.
"Do me a special favor",I asked.
"Since you have given me land in the Negeb
give me also springs of water."
My father nodded and made the gift.

So the Lower and the Upper Springs became ours.
to make the desert bloom..

All that took place some years ago.
Othniel and I have built a house
harvested several crops.
The Negeb blooms with water from the springs.

We are grateful to Yahweh for our land and our water.
Othniel and I have sons now
We are content to live on this good land.
flowing with milk and honey.

Think about these things...
Achsah

The land was precious to Achsah and her husband, Othniel. They cherished it. Jewish law stipulated that fields should lie fallow after seven years of use.

Land demands stewardshiip to help it be productive. Our food comes to us from the land. Yet our country sees large quantities of farmland pass each year into suburban development.

How can you show a love for the land? Here are some suggestions: plant a garden, learn how to compost your own yard and kitchen waste. Join a conservation group, hug a tree. God needs people who walk on the earth with a gentle tread.

A Glimpse of... Orpah

What can we say about Orpah? She appears in the first chapter of Ruth and then we never see her again. Like Ruth, she is a Moabite, who marries an alien husband from Bethlehem and becomes a childless widow.

Naomi, her mother-in-law, urges her to return to her home. Orpah sees that as the only solution. With the death of her father she can give support to her widowed mother, just as she has supported Naomi. She takes for granted that Ruth will accompany her. However, Ruth has come to love Naomi and chooses what she hopes will be a better, if uncertain future.

Orpah in this story acts as a foil for Ruth. Orpah chooses the expected action: to return to what she has always known. Ruth makes the extraordinary and unexpected choice. Even though Orpah chooses the familiar way, she also has wishes and dreams which she hopes to see fulfilled in her return home to Moab.

PRAYER: Dear God, give shelter for the widow and orphan: help us to be sensitive and understanding of the people in our midst who are different from us. Help us to show them that we know they also are your children. Amen.

Orpah

Ruth 1

I am all alone now.
Ruth and Naomi have begun their trek:
Naomi to her homeland
Ruth to an uncertain future.
Now I must find my way
back to my mother's house.

I love them both
and hate to leave them,
but why should I go to a foreign land?
I'm surprised at Ruth's decision.
I had hoped we could travel together.

How quickly these ten years have flown!
Naomi and her husband, Elimelech,
first came to Moab when the famine
struck hard in Bethlehem.
They were farming folk, like us,
with two sons, Mahlon and Chilion.

Elimelech died not long after they arrived.
Now Naomi had no man: a widow with two sons.
She urged her sons to marry,
and since there were no Hebrew women here,
Mahlon and Chilion came to our village.
Chilion asked my father for my hand
and Mahlon found Ruth to his liking.

We both were married and lived in harmony.
We had no children, though.
Naomi mourned that sad fact in her heart;
Ruth and I shared many things,
but neither of us talked of being barren.

Suddenly disease made us widows.
Illness took our husbands so quickly:
one day they were well,
the next, we wore our widow's garments.

Naomi mourned the most because her loss
was double—she had lost sons and a husband.
She felt alone within the Moab land,
so through her grief she analysed her choices,
thinking that someone back in Bethlehem
could find a humble place for her to stay
and work for her to do in her old age.
Word reached us soon that crops were good again
in Bethlehem. Naomi dreamed of home.

She gathered all her clothing, a few treasures
she'd saved; announced that she was going home.
Ruth and I suggested we escort her.
(The roads were no place for a woman of her age.)
Naomi shook her head, kissed us goodbye.

We cried at parting protesting her action.
But she asked us:
"Why do you want to come with me?
Do you think I can have sons again for you to marry?
Go back home, for I am too old to get married again.
Even if I thought there was still hope
and so got married tonight and had sons,
would you wait until they had grown up?
Would this keep you from marrying someone else?
No, my daughters, you know that's impossible.
The Lord has turned against me,
and I feel very sorry for you." (TEV)

She persuaded me. My father died while I was away.
I could go back and help my widowed mother.
With one last hug, I bade Naomi farewell,
then paused to see if Ruth would come with me.

But she was crying on Naomi's breast.
Naomi begged her to go home with me,
but Ruth replied:
"Don't ask me to leave you!
Wherever you go, I will go;
wherever you live, I will live.
Your people will be my people,
and your God will be my God.
Wherever you die, I will die,

and that is where I will be buried.
May the Lord's worst punishment come upon me
if I let anything but death separate me from you."

My eyes blurred tears when I looked at those two.
What future loomed for Ruth among those Hebrews?
I hear those folk despise all foreigners.

May our gods deal kindly with you, my sister.
May no harm come to you.

Now the road stretches forward to my village
and I must travel back to my own home.
My mother may not welcome one more mouth,
 to feed, but I am strong. I'll prove my worth to her.
I can work all day in the fields. I'll clean our home.
I'll look around the village too,
Perhaps some man has lost his wife
and needs a woman to care for his children.
Perhaps another husband and—a babe?

Think about these things...
Orpah

Orpah chose a familiar path; Ruth an uncertain one.

How do you make choices? Do you ruminate on them and place one choice against another? Do you choose impulsively and hope for the best? Do you ask God to help you choose and be with you as you walk into the distant country, or to the familiar landscape, which may have been changed by time?

A Glimpse of... Hannah

This story concerns a family triangle. Hannah, the first wife of Elkanah, was barren. Penninah, the second wife, bore many children to Elkanah. Hannah was loved greatly by her husband even though she had no children. Such a triangle of relationships makes for difficult living.

Penninah realized that she was a wife who was only cherished for her children. Jealousy made her provoke Hannah continually.

This situation came to a head when the family went to Shiloh for the yearly sacrifice. Hannah refused to join in the festivities that accompanied the rites. Instead, she went to the temple to pour out her soul before the Lord.

Eli, the priest noticed her silent praying. Custom at that time dictated that prayers be prayed out loud. Eli leaped to the conclusion that Hannah was drunk and chided her about it. But Hannah explained herself, and then Eli gave his blessing.

Hannah, feeling her prayer had been answered, went to her quarters and ate and drank.

Hannah's prayer was a bargaining with God: "if you give me a son, I'll give him to you for life". From Hannah's womb came the baby who would become the prophet, Samuel, who crowned two kings and was a force against idolatry for the Hebrew people.

PRAYER: Dear God: help us remember Hannah when we are provoked. Rather than answer the person in an unkindly way, may we turn to you in prayer to bear the angry words and not let them change us. Amen.

Hannah

1 Samuel 1:1-20

I fold his linen ephod lovingly
and pack them with his other clothes.
Tomorrow the family journeys to Shiloh
for the annual sacrifice.
Tomorrow I will see my first born son again!

I will go willingly from Ramah this time
not like the year when I despaired of life.
He will soon be five years old
growing both in body and in spirit under Eli's care.

This year I will worship joyfully
singing my praises to the Lord
Not like six years ago when we travelled to Shiloh.
I carried a load of grief from years before
- an aching pain that would not go away.

Elkanah, my husband, had another wife, Peninnah,
who regularly presented him with offspring.
I had no babe—a mortal sin for women— not to bear
a baby meant you had no future and no status.
That stigma hurt me, but Peninnah's cutting words hurt more.
His second wife despised me and made no secret of her hate.
Oh, how she plagued me! But I held my peace
believing her venom came from jealousy of me
because Elkanah favored me above her.
This provocation went along for years
I felt shrivelled as a woman -- dross best thrown away.
Elkanah failed to see my depth of sorrow.

That day in Shiloh, he told me he loved me best of all;
even gave me double portions of the sacrivice,
but no food or drink passed my lips that day.
I only wept and would not be consoled.

"Hannah, why do you weep?" Elkanah said.
"Why do you not eat?
Why is your heart sad?
Am I not more to you than ten sons?"
I shook my head at him - he did not understand.

34   Glimpses of Biblical Women & Other Poems

I left our quarters; journeyed to the temple.
I could not speak out loud - my heart was breaking -
so I wept and prayed silently. Pouring my heart's
desires before the Lord.

"Oh Lord of Hosts," I prayed, "If only you will look down
on the misery of your servant, and remember me
and not forget your servant,
but will give to your servant a male chld
then I will set him before you as a Nazarite
until the day of his death.
He shall drink neither wine nor intoxicants
and no razor shall touch his head."

Eli, the priest, came near and said to me
"How long will you make a drunken spectacle of yourself?
Put away your wine."

But I answered him, knowing that the custom
was to pray out loud and shout to the Lord.

"No my Lord, I am a woman deeply troubled.
I have drunken neither wine nor strong drink
but I have been pouring out my soul before the Lord.
Do not regard your servant as a worthless woman,
for I have been speaking out of my great anxiety
and vexation all this time."

His manner changed. His face softened and he smiled.
"Go in peace; the God of Israel grant the petition
you have made of him."

I bowed my head to him, acknowledging his words...
"Let your servant find favor in your sight," I said.

With a light heart I went back to our rooms
suddenly very hungry and no longer grieving.
I was sure the Lord had heard my plea.

After worship the next morning we journeyed back to Ramah.
I kept the hope that Eli's words had given me
and in due time I knew I was with child.

A Glimpse of Biblical Women & Other Poems

I had not forgotten my vow to the Lord.
This precious child did not belong to me;
so when Samuel was three, we went to Shiloh.
We sacrificed a bull, fulfilling all the rites.
Then we gave our son to Eli.

I said to the priest, "Oh my lord, As you live, my lord
I am the woman who was standing here in your presence
praying to the Lord. For this child I prayed;
and the Lord granted me the petition I made to him.
Therefore I have lent him to the Lord;
as long as he lives, he is given to the Lord."
I kissed my son and left him there with Eli.

Now every year I bring my boy a robe and other clothes
When we come to sacrifice.

The Lord has blessed my home.
I know another baby grows beneath my heart.
Peninnah's ragging has been silenced too.
She has no compelling cause to goad me further,
and I have made my peace with her at last.

Think about these things...
Hannah

The Bible is full of stories of barren women whom God loved and gave them children as a sign of his love. Think of the joy Hannah must have felt when her baby came. Then, three years later, she kept her promise to the Lord to give Samuel to the temple. Her gratitude for having a baby made her keep her promise.

What kind of promises do you make to God? Do you keep them?

A Glimpse of....Abigail

Abigail is the wife of Nabal, the Calebite. His name in Hebrew means "fool". Nabal is a rich man with thousands of sheep and goats, but not blessed with good sense.

Nabal's men are shearing sheep. David sends some of his men to help protect the sheep shearers. For this so-called "protection", David believes he and his men should be invited to the feast after the work is done. So David sends some men to Nabal with this request. Instead of offering hospitality to them, as Hebrew custom demanded, Nabal rebuffs them.

When the men returned to David with their story, David was incensed. "Every man strap on your sword," he cries. He and his men plan to annihilate every male in the area.

Nabal's young men, fearing the worst after Nabal's rebuff of David, tell Abigail the story. Quickly she springs into action, assembling bread, wine, figs, grain, raisins; loads these all on donkeys and heads toward David's army. Wisely, she does not tell her husband.

PRAYER: How often, God, could we avert unhappiness or tragedy if we could be sensitive in the midst of discord. Enlighten our minds, so we may become peace makers and protectors of shalom.   Amen.

Abigail

1 Samuel 25:14-36

"What is this terrible truth you tell me, Reuben?
My husband ignored the help of David's men
refusing them an invitation to our feast,
after they had guarded the sheep herders well.
Another case of foolish mouth on Nabal's part!
Tell me, where are David's men now?"

"They left," Reuben said,,
"soon after the encounter with Nabal."

Then they would soon return to David's camp
and spread the news of that ill- mannered man I married.
I hear that David has a will to match his ruddy hair.
"Quick, round up the servants, we have work to do.
I must be down the road before he comes."

How we scurried!. First donkeys were led out
and burdened with loads of parched grain,
clusters of raisins, cakes of figs, skins of wine,
as well as five dressed sheep and two hundred loaves of
 bread.
Our servants led the donkeys. We went to meet our foe
who would be the next king of the land,
fearful that the army David led might appear before we'd
 put some distance from our farm.

I heard them marching before I saw their faces.
Suddenly our progress was impeded
by a horde of David's soldiers.
David's face was red, his breathing shallow.

I quickly dismounted from my beast
falling at his feet, I bowed to him.

> "Upon me alone, my lord, be the guilt;
> please let your servant speak in your ears,
> and hear the words of your servant.
> My lord, do not take seriously
> this illmannered fellow, Nabal;
> for as his name is, so is he.

A Glimpse of Biblical Women & Other Poems

Nabal is his name, and folly is with him;
But I, your servant, did not see the young men
of my lord whom you sent.

Now then, my lord, as the Lord lives,
and as you yourself live,
since the Lord has restrained you from bloodguilt
and from taking vengeance with your own hand,
now let your enemies and those who seek to do evil
to my lord be like Nabal,
and now let this present that your servant
has brought to my lord be given to the young men
who follow my lord.
Please forgive the trespass of your servant;
for the Lord will certainly make my lord
a sure house, because my lord is fighting
the battles of the Lord;
and evil shall not be found in you
so long as you live.
If anyone should rise up to pursue you
and to seek your life,
the life of my lord shall be bound
in the bundle of the living
under the care of the Lord your God;
but the lives of your enemies
he shall sling out as from the hollow of a sling.
When the Lord has done to my lord
according to all the good that he has spoken
concerning you, and has appointed you
prince over Israel, my lord shall have no cause
of grief, or pangs of conscience,
for having shed blood without cause
or for having saved himself.
And when the Lord has dealt well with my lord,
then remember your servant."

David listened to my plea, his features softened.
Smiling at me he said,
   "Blessed be the Lord,
   the God of Israel, who sent you to meet me today.
   Blessed be your good sense and blessed be you,
   who have kept me today from bloodguilt
   and from avenging myself by my own hand.
   For as surely as the Lord, the God of Israel lives,

who has restrained me from hurting you,
unless you had hurried and come to meet me,
truly by morning there would not have been left
to Nabal so much as one male."

We relieved the donkeys of their burdens
David's men helped, so eager were they for the bounty.
They could have their own feast
instead of the planned bloodbath.

Then David said to me,
    "Go up to your house in peace,
    see, I have heeded your voice,
    and I have granted your petition."

I went home lighter that I'd come
and with a lighter heart.
I was content I had averted tragedy.
Tomorrow I would tell Nabal the story,
and see what he would say.

Think about these things...
Abigail

How many of us would have been as quick to avert bloodshed as Abigail was? She knew David's men would be hungry and tired. A good meal would cool the blood lust and avert tragedy.

How do you show hospitality? Do you have meals that are simple, so the time can be devoted to conversation instead or rich food? Do you have a pleasant place where guests are at ease? Is your home a welcoming place? Do you listen to your guests in a way they know you care? All these actions proclaim hospitality. When have you had a guest when you and she enjoyed one another's company and were enriched by the fellowship you shared? What made that time special?

A Glimpse of... Huldah

This story takes place during the reign of King Josiah of Judah. He was concerned that Judah slipped more and more into paganism, worshipping the Asherahs and Baals. During the time he began his destruction of these practices Josiah commanded that the Temple be repaired. Kings before him had neglected the Temple, and even though money had been raised for its repair, nothing had been done.

Josiah commissioned the best workmen and ordered their payment from the Temple funds. During that time a scroll was discovered by the priests. They began to read it, and finally it was taken to the king. When Josiah heard the words of the scroll he tore his clothing in repentence. He sent his priests to Huldah, the prophetess, to inquire of the Lord and bring word back to the king.

Huldah lived in the western hills of the Second Quarter of Jerusalem. Her husband, Shallum, took care of the wardrobe of the temple. Huldah interpreted the message of the scroll in the familiar way of prophets: Thus says the Lord.

What was on this scroll that caused such a commotion? Basically, it was Chapters 12-26 from the Book of Deuteronomy. Women had a role as prophets at that time, but their accomplishments were not as highlighted in scripture as were those of Jeremiah, Isaiah or Ezekiel.

Still if we read between the lines we can appreciate that Huldah's work did not go unnoticed. The reforms Josiah instituted continued after Huldah proclaimed God's word written in the scroll. Though the reforms did not last and doom did descend, Huldah remains as one who proclaimed God's judgement on idolatry, injustice and unrighteousness.

PRAYER: O God of Justice, look upon our culture and show us the idols we worship. Reform and release us from our sins so we may serve you in truth and faithfulness. Amen.

Huldah

2 Kings 22 and 2 Chronicles 34

A deputation at my door—
what brings these priests and high officials here?
They tell me they brought an ancient scroll
uncovered recently during the Temple renovation.

I wish them well, invite them in
and usher them into my sitting room.
Five men come upon a solemn errand,
their bodies tense and their demeanor grave.

"Wife of Shallum," they say,
respecting my husband's temple role.
I nod and seat them, call for some refreshment,
They shake their heads: "There is no time," they say.

Hilkiah, Ahikam, Achbor,
Shaphan and Asaiah sit restlessly
intent upon their errand.

"The king has sent us to you
to inquire of the Lord for him,
and all those left in Israel and Judah
concerning the words of the book that has been found.
For the wrath of the Lord that is poured out on us
is great, because our ancestors did not keep
the word of the Lord, to act in accordance
with all that is written in this book."

I reached my hand to grasp the greasy scroll
—vellum it was—and crumbling at the edge.
My body tingled from the touch.
This was no common scroll!

They leave. I bend my head over faded characters.
Words come alive to me: Our Yahweh speaks these words.
I read until my eyes could see no more,
then light the oil lamp and read again.
Surely it is a holy afternoon,
feeling so close to Yahweh through the words.
I am transfixed—all time seems meaningless.
Yet as I read, my heart despairs

I think about the asherahs on the hills,
the temple prostitutes, the wasted lives,
the violence of the wealthy toward the poor.

I wept that night for my Jerusalem:
so heedless of the truth,
consumed by rites and privilege.
Would the people turn to Yahweh as Josiah hoped?
Was the pollution in the land too great?

Come morning the five men return to me
watching with veiled eyes to hear my words.
So I, with heavy heart began my oracle:
> "Thus says the Lord: I will indeed bring disaster
> upon this place and upon its inhabitants,
> all the curses that are written in the book
> that was read before the king of Judah.
> Because they have forsaken me
> and have made offerings to other gods,
> so that they have provoked me to anger
> with all the works of their hands,
> my wrath will be poured out on this place
> and will not be quenched.
> But as to the king of Judah,
> who sent you to inquire of the Lord,
> thus shall you say to him:
> Regarding the words that you have heard,
> because your heart was penitent
> and you humbled yourself before God
> when you heard his words against this place
> and its inhabitants,
> and you have humbled yourself before me,
> and have torn your clothes and wept before me,
> I also have heard you, says the Lord.
> I will gather you to your ancestors
> and you shall be gathered to your grave in peace;
> our eyes shall not see all the disaster
> that I will bring on this place."

They take the scroll and leave without a word,
shoulders sagging from my weighty message.
Soon proclamation comes from the king
that Passover will be celebrated—that holy day
when freedom came to Jews, and they were spared
the evil curse of death upon their offspring.

A Glimpse of Biblical Women & Other Poems

So the whole city celebrates Passover
as Josiah, our repentent king commands.
For many who had never heard of Passover
the words seemed strange upon their ears;
they feel uneasy with the liturgy.

Josiah still continues his destruction
of all the high places where the false gods
are worshipped, knocking them down and
grinding bones to scatter
upon the graves of those who worshipped Baal.

May Yahweh look kindly on his people
and give them strength to face the days ahead.

Think about these things...
Huldah

How do you deliver bad news? Huldah gently told the men the results of their nation's apostasy. Josiah would be spared because he had turned to the Lord, but the nation would be destroyed. The moral decay in the land led to uneasy alliances with powerful leaders of other countries.
Eventually, the kingdom would fall and the people would be carried to Babylon.

What do you do when you see someone breaking the law or flaunting society's standards? Do you confront them or are you afraid of being mocked? What do you believe God wants you to do in such a situation?

New Testament

A Glimpse of... Mary & Elizabeth

Mary must have travelled with a company from Nazareth on her journey to see Elizabeth. The roads were too full of ruffians for a woman to travel alone.

She must have had time to ponder what had happened to her. What it all meant. This baby would change her life.

What would people think of her? She did not look pregnant on her journey out but after six months with Elizabeth, there would be no doubt she was pregnant.

How could she explain to Joseph that she had not been unfaithful to him? He had promised to marry her on her return, but what if he had changed his mind?

PRAYER: God, who made the barren woman glad with child and filled Mary's womb with our Lord, help us accept your grace when it enters our lives. Amen.

Mary & Elizabeth

Luke 1:39-56

Three months they spent together
cooking meals, washing dishes, making beds
doing common chores all women do.

Elizabeth the six month mother to be
Mary hardly showing.
Both of them transformed
by Gabriel's pronouncements
of their future.

The house was still.
Zachariah could not speak.
though he gestured meaningfully
from time to time
and they dared not serve his dinner late.

What did they say to each other
after the first shock of recognition?
Whatever women say to each other
when in a "delicate condition."

Elizabeth shared her wonder joyfully
still amazed that after year on year
of being barren, she was with child.

Mary's happiness was tinged with apprehension.
It had all happened so quickly
the angel spoke to her
and suddenly she felt impregnated
but she was raised as a dutiful girl
"Let it be as you say."

She remembered the angel's words
"Do not be afraid."

How many hours they sat together
remembering their pasts
speaking of their futures
What would their futures hold?
and how would they behave
when such a wonder came to them?

Elizabeth prayed prayers of thankfulness,
and Mary wondered fearfully at her reception
when she returned to Nazareth.

Think about these things...
Mary & Elizabeth

Two women — one old and one young. They did what women have done across the centuries. They talked, laughed and cried together and found comfort and strength from their relationship.

Do you have a woman friend or belong to a woman's group that meets regularly? None of us is strong enough to bear life's trials alone. It may be a Bible study group, or a group that shares meals together. Whatever it is, this community of women is carrying on Elizabeth and Mary's pattern.

A Glimpse of... Elizabeth

There are many stories of barren women in both the Old and the New Testaments: Sarah, Rachel, Hannah and more. Into each of these women's lives comes a child after agonizing years of waiting. Each birth proves God's power.

Zechariah, Elizabeth's husband, was a priest who belonged to the order of Abijah. His name was picked by lot to serve in the temple. Elizabeth had a priestly family background also and was a woman of faith. Through all the years of sniggering laughter or ostracism from other more fertile women, she maintains her composure and her deep seated belief in God's mercy.

The silence imposed upon her husband after he returns from his experience in the Temple adds another burden to her life, for they are the only two people who know the secret.. Imagine the joy of her first morning sickness when she realizes God's promise to Zechariah!

She does not gloat as her body gives evidence of the coming birth. She lives joyfully each day of her pregnancy, knowing she carries a special gift from God.

PRAYER: God of great surprises: we thank you for the example of Elizabeth. May we cherish our children as your wonders, and so model the gospel that it becomes reality in their lives. Amen.

Elizabeth

Luke 1:1-25

When I remember the shame I felt!
Barren, barren for years and years.
No baby's body pulled out from my womb.

Across the years my prayers availed me nothing.
"Give me a son, O Lord," I'd cry.
"I'll dedicate his life to you
even as Hannah did of old."
But years crept by and nothing happened.

Then last year the lot fell to Zechariah
to go up to Jerusalem to serve in the Temple rites.
There an angel met him and told a tale
about our wondrous future.
But Zechariah disbelieved the angel
and was cursed with muteness
for not accepting truth that God could turn
old women, like me, into mothers.

When Zechariah returned, he could not speak a word,
yet I saw in his face, his staring eyes
that terrible, wonderful news that muted him.
I did not blame him for his disbelief.
How can it be that God would open wombs
long closed and long forgotten?

The townsfolk, noting Zechariah's plight,
asked silly questions, but I turned a heel.
We took up our living as before
yet something made us extra loving,
though we had always loved each other well.
At night I'd snuggle close to Zechariah,
whispering my hopes and fears in secret.
We kept the knowledge close between us
hoping angel's words were really true.

Slowly my body changed, the baby grew,
but when one's been the butt of ridicule
one does not give one's scoffers any privilege.
For several months I stayed within my doors.
But one day cousin Mary came with wondrous news
about a babe she carried—the Messiah all the Hebrews
were anticipating—who would free us from the rulers over us.
When I beheld her, my own baby kicked.
We held each other through our tears of joy.
At last my secret could be hid no longer
and neighbor women came to me rejoicing.

I labored long, but I did not regret it.
I would have died to bring this son to birth.
But I did not die, and on this special day
of baby's naming and his circumcision,
the priest directs his gaze at Zechariah
and asks the usual question "He will have your name?"
but knowing Zechariah can't assent, I call out
"No, his name is John". Zechariah nods,
scratching upon his wooden writing block,
    "His name is John."
So John is named
and so he claims his heritage
foretold by angels many months ago.

The priest cuts foreskin carefully
and only at the end
does John begin to cry.

I hold him close to me.
What will become of you, my holy one?
For you are promised to the Lord for life.
Dark shadows surely fleet across your path...
But I won't think about that now.
As I touch his tiny head
and smooth his burnished hair,
my world is graced with miracles ineffable.
Blessed beyond all women is Elizabeth.
Blessed with a squealing child to love at last.

Think about these things...
Elizabeth

Women's role in Bible times was to be the bearer of children. Elizabeth's wish for a child came years after she had given up all hope.

Are you struggling with being childless? Or have you chosen to be child free in your household? How does God call all adults to parent young people in our communities?

A Glimpse of... Mary & the Wise Men

The star that guided the wise men is said to have appeared at Jesus' birth. To travel the distance from Persia to Judea would take the wise men a long time. In our Christmas worship services we hear all the stories at the same time. But not all the events took place at the same time. These stories do not blend together. One gospel tells part of the story; another tells another part. Each story in itself is a jewel.

Jesus may have been a toddler when the wise men came to bring their gifts. Mary must have been amazed to be honored by such gifts.

PRAYER: O God, help us to love children the way Mary must have loved Jesus. Amen

Mary & the Wise Men

Matthew 2:1-12

I was not prepared. How could I be?
Three men robed as kings at my door.

Jesus and I are alone. Joseph is working in the town.
I fear to open the door
yet what can I do?
Their faces look kind.
They also look tired. They must have travelled far.
Perhaps I can help them find their destination.
I welcome them in and ask if I may help them.

But I soon learned that we were their destination.
Jesus toddles across the floor, wide eyed
and clings to my skirt.

The three men bow low and ask to enter our house.
They have gifts for us!
When they see Jesus peeking out from behind my skirt
  they fall on their knees
praying in their own language.
They offer us their gifts: gold, frankincense and myrrh.

"Have you come far?" I ask to fill the silence
for they adore my son and stand enraptured.
"Many miles", said the one who offered gold.
"We have come to see the King of the Jews."

Jesus pokes his head out from behind me.
They smile at him; he smiles back.
Slowly he closes the distance between the men and me.
He touches their fine clothing, dusty though it is.
He laughs and they laugh too.

I ask them to sit down; we have few chairs.
They sit upon the sleeping mat.
Jesus climbs into the lap of the dark man
  and snuggles closely
resting his curly head upon the man's shoulder.
The other two kings watch in fascination.

Now they have gone.
I am left amazed again
like the wonder I felt when Gabriel, the angel,
told me about my unborn child
who would become the Son of God.

These past two years have been so filled with wonders.
Now these gifts honor my small son.
What can it mean? Will he be a prophet when he's grown?

Think about these things...
Mary & the Wise Men

We do not know about Jesus's childhood, except for the episode in the temple. This poem is an attempt to visualize what his babyhood might have been.

Can you imagine Jesus as a curious toddler? What things did he like to do?

A Glimpse of... Anna

All the Bible tells us about Anna is contained in one short paragraph. Her story follows Simeon's blessing of Jesus as "a light for revelation to the Gentiles and for glory to your people Israel." Anna is not quoted.

She had reached an advanced age at the time of our story. Married for seven years, then a widow, she was 84 years old when she met the baby Jesus. She spent each day in the outer court of the temple because women were not allowed into the Holy of Holies. She prayed and fasted.

Mary and Joseph came to the temple with the baby Jesus to make the sacrifice Jewish law demands of each firstborn. Anna met them and recognized the importance of this child. Simeon had the same exaltation when he held Jesus in his arms, but his response came as thanks for the gift given to an old man who could now die in peace. Anna's response, though she too was aged, became a proclamation of God's gift to all who had been looking for change and redemption in Jerusalem. Anna, as so mamy women who came after her, could not keep still with the good news of Jesus' birth.

PRAYER: We are old, middle aged and young women, O God. Whatever our age, help us tell the Jesus story with joy and an anticipation of a better world that we can build with your help. Amen.

Anna

Luke 2:36-38

Aach! my old bones!
So many years here in the Temple
still, I can fast and pray to our God.
These many years I've done so,
since I was a widow after seven years of marriage
until now when I am eighty four
and will continue praising God until I'm in my grave.

The times are hard, but I still believe
there will be a redemption for Jerusaleem
even though we are governed by conquerors.
We've suffered much as a people
in wars and exile and now the Roman rulers
who employ Hebrew puppets to do their will.

When will the Messiah come? Who knows?

In the Courtyard of the Women I see a couple
who have brought their newborn to be dedicated.
The woman is so young - her first, I'd guess.
The man is older, sheltering his wife.
As they pass the child to the priest, I see his face.
My heart beats faster.
Can it be Messiah in the flesh?
Many children have been dedicated here,
but none like this child.

After the dedication ceremony I draw near.
His little hand uncurls and curls around my finger.
Such a lovely child!

They move away, their sacrifice complete.
I stand transfixed a moment, then in joy
a joy I cannot keep in check
I praise our God for what I've seen today.
and I must share my news with others.
God has come near, not on a chariot bright
but in a little baby's curled finger.

Think about these things...
Anna

Anna lives a life completely dedicated to God. She recognizes the baby Jesus as the Messiah. The meeting is an occasion to praise God and hope for better days to come in the religious life of the Jews.

Each child born has promise of hope for the world. How may we help children to fulfill that hope?

A Glimpse of... the Woman with a Hemorrhage

Blood was an important part of the sacrificial life of the Hebrews. Goats and sheep were sacrificed on the altar at the temple and their blood used to wash away sins.

The purity laws pertaining to women had a different view of blood. Women were not clean when they were menstrating. After the flow ceased the woman must be purified before she could resume her place in society. Imagine how you would feel if your flow never stopped, but went on for years and years. The woman became an outcast to society, not able to associate normally with other people. This is the situation of this woman who wishes desperately to be healed.

PRAYER: Healing God, we may not have dilemmas such as the woman with the hemorrhage did, but we need to be healed also. Transform our attitudes toward people who are homeless, poor or hungry. Teach us compassion like Jesus taught with the woman. Amen.

The Woman with a Hemorrhage

Mark 5:25-34

Blood!
Red, sticky, smelly mucus- laden blood,
leaking like a sieve from me.

I have been like this for many years
feeling weak, helpless and shunned
by the community.

Doctors only shook their heads and took my money
but gave me no relief.
I never gave up hope though
it drove me all these years.
Hope drove me to join this band
of village people when someone cried
"Jesus is coming.
The one who heals the sick
and gives sight to the blind."
Perhaps, I thought, he could heal me.

I would not be so bold as to accost him
as he walked. No, no, if only I could
touch his garment then I would be healed.

So I hurried as best I could to the place
  where Jesus walked.
Fighting my way through the crowd
I finally saw him and crept forward.
There! I touched the hem of his robe
OH, what a change!
I am standing straight again
I am not bleeding.
I could hardly believe it.

Just then Jesus stopped.
He asked his disciples "Who touched me?"
His friends chuckled at the absurdity of his query.
"Look at all these people," they said,
"How can we tell who touched you?"

But Jesus insisted someone had touched him.
He felt the power leave him.

I could hide no more.
I came to him on my knees
not looking in his face
tears bathing my cheeks.

"I touched you," I said.

Jesus' hand lifted my chin
so I had to look into his eyes.
So warm, so unjudgemental.
I poured out my story
and as I talked
the years of pain drained away
like dirty bath water.

After years and years of bleeding
I had almost given up,
but I thought if I can only touch
the hem of your garment
I would be healed--and I was!

Jesus smiled at me.
"Go, my daughter. Your faith has made you well."

Think about these things...
Woman with a Hemorrhage

Persistent illness that never is cured can drain a woman's spirit and energy. She was an outcast because of her bleeding. Somehow she summoned enough strength to fight her way to Jesus' side.

Have you been as desperate as this woman? What did you do to change your situation? Imagine the release of anxiety she feels now she will be an accepted member of society.

A Glimpse of... Herodias

In this story we view court intrigue with its deadliest consequences. Herodias was a child of her epoch, when the Herodian court paid only lip service to the Jewish laws and courted the Greek lifestyle.

The wife of Philip Herod, Herodias fell in love with Herod Antipas, divorced her husband. and married Herod. She was forty years old at the time of her second marriage. Jewish law prohibited a woman marrying her husband's brother when the husband still lived. John the Baptist kept reminding Herod of that infraction during their talks in the dungeon. Herod, a thoroughly secular person, was fascinated by John, even though he didn't understand him. Herod tried to protect John by keeping him captive.

Herodias hated John for his disapproval of her marriage. That hatred led to seething revenge, anger and then plotting to kill John. In Salome, her daughter, she found an unknowing cohort.

Herodias was not an enviable woman. Belonging to the royal family, she was used to getting her way, even if it involved someone's death.

But killing John did not stop his message. Herodias would have been surprised years later, when she and her husband had been exiled to Europe by the Emperor, Gaius, that disciples of John would still be worshipping in many countries of the Middle East.

PRAYER: Merciful God, We get angry and frustrated. Take the energy of our anger and teach us to use it in useful ways: to brighten the lives of our families; to lighten the load of poor people; and to protest injustice. Amen

Herodias

Mark 6:17-29

That coarse man,
with shaggy beard and beast's skins for clothing!

I saw him from my window
when Herod brought him here to Tiberias
I thought Herod brought him to behead him
but as the days and months passed
I realized that Herod was protecting him.

Herod would sit for hours
like a stupid schoolboy
listening to his tirades.
Our marriage was anathema to John,
He often told Herod about our "sin".
As if he had a right to rebuke us!

My hatred of John grew
eating like a cancer in my soul,
kept hidden from my husband's curious eyes.
I must be sly, like Herod,
if I was to achieve my goal.

So I bided my time
until a banquet was announced for Herod's birthday.
He invited all the top officials of Galilee,
officers of the army and the leading citizens.

Herod can be sly and canny
but when he has a belly full of wine
discretion slips off like a snake's old skin.
That was what I counted on.

Salome danced for the assembled company
her body lithe and sinuous.
A vision of beauty and grace.
She stirs men's blood by her dancing.
Their hearts beat staccato time
their faces masks of lust.

When Salome's performance reached crescendo
Herod clapped his hand and spoke in blurry voice
"Ask for whatever you wish, and I will give it
...even half of my kingdom."

Salome rushed to me, not knowing of my plan.
"What shall I ask for?" she asked me.
"The head of John the Baptizer."

She rushed back to the king and said:
"I want you to give me at once
the head of John the Baptist on a plattter."

Herod, shocked out of his stupor looked at her,
then at his guests all silent and waiting.

"Call a soldier of the guard," he yelled in strangled voice
and when the solider came he ordered John's beheading.

The banquet's gaity stopped, few spoke except in whispers.
Herod tried to play the host, but failed badly.

At last the door opened and the soldier entered
carrying a platter on which the head of John rested.

Salome bowed low, acknowledging the present
and carried the platter to my room.

So here we meet at last, John.
though we can hardly hold a conversation.
Your eyes bore into me as if alive,
but they do not move.
Stare on, old man!
I have the last word now.

Think about these things...
Herodias

Spoiled, wilful people insist on their own way. Herodias' hatred of John led her to sanction murder. As first, John's disapproval of her divorce seemed of little consequence, but as the days and months passed, she saw her husband responding to John, even though Herod was not a religious person.

Anger, unchecked, can lead to more dangerous sins. How do you react when you are angry? Denial, shouting or cold hate? Honest anger is an emotion common to all humans. What we do with our anger determines our faith or lack of it. Do we not let the sun go down on our anger?

A Glimpse of... the woman caught in adultery

The title of this story conjures up an image of a bird caught in a snare. Whatever passion led the woman to commit a sin deserving stoning, is not the focus of the story. Jesus is the one the scribes and Pharisees hope will fall into their trap. The woman may have already been accused and the crowd only brings her to Jesus to see what he will say. If he forgives her, he has violated the Mosaic law. If he deems her guilty, he's in trouble with the Roman rulers.

In their haste to trap Jesus, however, the scribes and Pharisees have overlooked two important tenets of the Mosaic Law; two witnesses, exclusive of the husband, were required to prove guilt. None were present. Neither was the man who had been her partner, who also was to be stoned..

This story has a parallel to the story of paying taxes to the Roman emperor in Matthew 22:15-22. Jesus answered the Pharisees'question that time with another question. This time Jesus is silent.

Jesus' action of drawing in the dirt focuses the attention of the crowd on him, and not on the woman. He realizes she is only a pawn in the religious leader's game.

PRAYER: Forgive us our sins, Compassionate One. Help us to be strong and to walk in the way of righteousness. Amen.

Woman caught in adultery

John 8:1-11

I draw my scanty clothes around my breasts
weary from a night of trial.
Why did they bring me to the Temple?
Where is my lover? I've not seen him
since the crowd broke into our room
and I was dragged away.

They shove me toward a man who sits there teaching
circled by a group of followers.
He stands as we approach as if expecting
such a crowd so early in the morning.

"We found this woman committing adultery." they shouted.
"She should be stoned."

The man says nothing. As I watch his expression
I see sorrow in his face as it searches the noisy crowd.
Then he bends down; looking away from the crowd.
His finger makes some movement in the dust
He seems unconcerned about their shouting,
but the questions still come falling on his ears
like stones meant for my body.

When he stand up he faces the crowd again.
"He who is without sin," he says,
"let him be the first to throw a stone at her."

Silence. A gasp of breath.
He bends once more, writing in the dirt.
One by one the men all slip away;
the older ones first. Soon the temple was empty
save for the two of us and his followers.

"Woman, where are they?" he says as he straightens up.
"Has no one condemned you?"
I answer "No one, sir."
"Neither do I condemn you. Go your way
and from now on do not sin again."

He hands me back a future.
Oh, a shaky one at that, but a chance.
My eyes began to shine at the prospect.
Yet from the sadness in the teacher's eyes
I sense he holds that promise out to my accusers also,
only they are not here.

Think about these things...
Woman caught in adultery

Jesus realized that the women's presence is a test of his credibility. So he remains silent. Her fear turns to hope as she watches the crowd disperse.

Our society glamorizes promiscuous sex without comment on the damage done to a marriage by adultery. How does one combat the allure of sex in TV and other media? How do we help young people to realize the results of their sexual adventures?

A Glimpse of... Procula

Procula is a privileged Roman matron, wife of Pontius Pilate, the prefect of the territory of Judea. Even though she is protected from contact with the ordinary people of Jerusalem, she feels the shock waves of conflict as her husband recounts his experiences when they share time together.

Procula has no love for the Jews. She sees them as a pious but blood-thirsty lot. She does not even know who Jesus is— only that she suffers from a dream that haunts her when morning comes.

Having little exposure to the intricicies of Jewish belief, she believes she can save Jesus' life. Even Pilate believes him innocent. But Pilate walks a political tightrope because of several unfortunate episodes with Jewish citizens. Therefore he is forced to bow to their wishes when they demand Jesus' crucifixion.

Procula's hope of saving Jesus went unmet. Though she finds it hard to rid herself of the dream, she turns her attention to caring for her husband when he returns from sentencing Jesus.

PRAYER: God of the stranger and the sojourner: we live among many folk we do not know well. Help us be sensitive and appreciative of their cultures and values. Amen.

Procula

Matthew 27:19

I woke in terror,
shivered till the room's shape came clear.
Such a strange dream!
Three crosses on a hill.
One man hung between two criminals.
I knew that man was innocent—
I know not how I knew—
Why would we crucify an innocent?

Thank the gods our stay in Antonia
lasts only till the Jewish holy days
are spent and crowds go home.
Each year brings some unrest
that Pilate must put down.
I pray no lives are lost in bitter combat,
though the city seems a boiling caldron.
I'll never understand these Jews.
They look so pious one minute,
then glad to stick a dirk
between your ribs another.

I tried to find Pilate
to tell him of my dream—
he listens to my visions—
but he had gone to tend affairs of state,
So I sent a message with Festus,
our trusted seervant:

"Do not hurt this man, Jesus.
He is a righteous man,
and I have suffered much
in a dream of him."
I bade Festus take my missive hence,
deliver to my husband and return.

I paced the floor.
I could not eat or drink.
Dreams tell us disturbing truths.
· The gods send messages through our dreams.

Long years ago I learned to trust their truth.
Surely my husband's decision will be just,
not swayed by what the Jews tell him.
Oh, but if his resolution crumbles
it would not be the first time.
He knows the Emperor has a watchful eye.
Too many crises mean recall to Rome.

"Festus, pray what means your sad face?
Did Pilate read the note?"
He nodded, then he shooks his head at me
and told me of the crowd
that shouted "crucify!"
"My master tried to change their minds
but they demanded a murderer be set free—
Barabbas, whom we know is guilty
three times over, an enemy of Rome!
My master washed his hands
and let the one named Jesus be led out.
He let them have their way.
They've taken him to Golgotha
to crucify with two state criminals."

I send the servants out and fold my hands.
Perhaps when this day's tragic circumstance
has passed, my dream will dissipate.
My husband will need comfort
when he comes to bury his head upon my breasts.
I'll kiss away his cares.
We'll lift a flagon till the vision of the crowd
begins to fade.

———————

Some say he was called King of the Jews,
yet I thought Jews owned no king except their god.

———————

Oh well, after I've soothed the prefect's guilt
about that Galilean
perhaps a stronger potion than my usual one
will bring me dreamless sleep.

Think about these things...
Procula

Wives of men in high places must often walk a tightrope between their values and the track their husbands move toward to a higher position. Procula's story, though small, reveals a woman who cares about someone she will never meet.

Her first loyalty, however, lies in the care of her husband. She submerges her fears in order to comfort him.

If you are in a powerless position, as Procula was, how can you adhere to your beliefs and still be true to your husband? Do you speak out against injustice or remain the silent woman?

A Glimpse of... Sapphira

The couple, Ananais and Sapphira, became members of the newly established group of Christians in Jerusalem. Probaby there were many folk who only came to be fed, grateful for a meal, with little understanding of the deep truths of Jesus' teachings. Ananais and Sapphira may have been such people, even though they were persons of means. Their commitment did not go deep enough. They saw only the outside of people's actions, not into their hearts.

The Old Testament has many examples of people who held out on the Lord and died. This is the first story in the New Testament of such an event. Luke wanted his readers to know the seriousness of commitments made to God.

In his story Luke tells us inadvertently something about the marriage of these two people. At a time when women had little say over family expenditures, Sapphira is consulted by her husband before giving the gift to the church. She is an equal with Ananais. So in death as in life, they share the same fate. A sad story of half-committed love.

PRAYER; God, who loves us as we are, may our love to you move from a half-love to a fire that burns within us and prompts us toward greater service. Amen.

Sapphira

Acts 5:1-11

I'm Ananais' wife.
We live in pleasant dwellings in Jerusalem.
Ours is a marraige strange to our neighbors.
I'm not held as bargained property,
but loved and consulted in his trade.
He likes my mind and values what I say,
confirms my beauty, as my name implies.

We joined this group
who talked about the risen Jesus—
a man who not too long ago had died
a shameful death upon a Roman cross.
His followers said he had come back to life
and death was dead forever. We relished the thought
and went to their group
meeting down a dusty street here in Jerusalem.

We found no past acquaintences
but met many widows and orphans
at the common meal (it may have been
their only daily food.)
The church was a community of friends
and all were welcome. All could come and share.
Those who prospered more were expected
to take care of those less fortunate.
We shared our food—oh, gladly, offered more
and were content to sup with new found friends.

Then Barnabas—that "son of encouragement"
they called him—whom everybody loved,
sold a field and brought the proceeds in
and laid them at the apostle's feet
and all were well pleased with his gracious gift.

Barnabas caused our downfall!
We prized our standing in the town
and thought that we could do the same as he.
When Ananias and I later talked,
he said "Let's sell that fallow field
and give the proceeds to the church."

A Glimpse of Biblical Women & Other Poems

I agreed, that field was no great boon.
We would do well to let the field go,
and when we brought our gift we would be loved
as Barnabas was loved.

So, we sold it, but in the bargain
we received more shekels than we'd ever dreamed,
and suddenly we thought of things we needed.
(Oh, we had heard the warnings from of old
about the folk who held out on the Lord
and died in ignominy, but that was long ago.)

So, Ananais took a portion from the sale
and went to Peter—he who is called "Rock".
I did not go till later, when meal time came
and Ananais had not returned.
I went to Peter asking after Ananais.

"Tell me," said Peter with a serious look,
whether you and your husband sold the land
for such and such a price.".
"Yes, that was the price," I said.

Then Peter said to me, "How is it that you have agreed
together to put the Spirit of the Lord
to the test. Look the feet of those
who have buried your husband are at the door,
and they will carry you out."

My heart began to flutter, then a cloud
as black as ebon floated over me
and I knew nothing else.

So now I sleep next to Ananais,
the sleep that lasts for all eternity,
and the money we intended for our selves
has passed to other hands. The grave has no regrets
but I have one: that Barnabas will be forever loved
and our names will become anathema!

Think about these things...
Sapphira

The story of Ananais and Sapphira highlights the corrosive effects of envy and greed. Sapphira and Ananais give their gift to bring honor to themselves, rather than to help feed the widows and orphans in the church. They envied Barnabas' good standing with church members without realizing that Barnabas had a spirit which made him loved. That was his gift, not the money.

Money is the one issue most of us do not want to talk about. The way we use our money gives us power. Is money an issue with which you would rather not deal?

A Glimpse of... A Widow of Joppa

This glimpse highlights the story of Tabitha (also known as Dorcas) and is told by one of the widows she helped. It is the only poem in the collection that does not describe a person named in Scripture.

Tabitha, a wealthy widow, and a Christian disciple, lived in Joppa. Her love for the Lord demonstrated itself in good works: she gave money to poverty striken widows as well as providing them clothing. Her death brought her philanthropy to a close.

The widow of Joppa represents all widows of ancient times. She is childless and poor. She becomes dependent upon Tabitha and accepts dependency as her role in life. She never takes an active part in her society. New possibilities for her life elude her. The shock of losing Tabitha and the miracle of her being restored to life provide the impetus she needs to see her life from a new perspective.

PRAYER: Protector and Comforter: we each see the world through narrow eyes of self interest. Broaden our view, stretch our understanding that we may see new possibilities for our lives through service to others. Amen.

A Widow of Joppa

Acts 9:36-43

Tabitha was a good woman.
She was a follower of The Way—
that new religion setting many afire in Judea.
Those people follow a man called Jesus
who died and came to life again, they say.

It all sounded too far-fetched for me,
but there must be something to it.
Tabitha lived her faith.
She didn't have to share her goods with us,
the widows of Joppa.
She felt no pinch, she had money to spare,
Many rich women think only of themselves.
But not Tabitha.

She made the finest clothing with her own hands.
She wove the cloth and made fine garments.
She seemed to know when extra wraps were needed,
and would slip a garment to us without show.
Oh, she was a fine woman!

But now, she's gone.
She died in the night,
her soul slipping away in the dark,
and this morning all I heard
was lamentation from the other widows.
We were so used to depending upon her.
Now that she's gone, what will become of us?

I wiped my tears. Practical matters first.
No use thinking only of my loss.
I could honor Tabitha as best I could.
The other women and I washed her body lovingly
and laid her on her bed.

Then the wailing began as custom dictated.
I did not wail, I was too numb with grief.
What would I do? I scarcely dared to think.
I had no one. My husband died some years ago;

we had no sons, I had no relatives.
I mourned for myself almost as much
as I wept for loss of Tabitha.

In the midst of the wailing a man appeared.
I did not know his face.
He shooed us out the door and closed it
  tight behind him.
His appearance took us all off guard.
We all fell silent.

"He's come to pray for Tabitha's soul,"
one woman guessed.

Another said his name was Peter,
one of the followers of the Jesus Way.

The door soon opened. Ah, a miracle!
Peter led our Tabitha on his arm.
Our tear-stained faces brightened into joy.
We could not speak—we could not say a word.

Then Tabitha, still smiling came down the stairs,
picked up her sewing as if nothing'd happened.

Something in me caught fire. I thought
of all the years I'd only asked and taken,
never given anything.
I'd felt free then to take dear Tabitha's gifts,
but now a miracle had happened. I saw
a woman come from death to life.
That miracle touched me
and I would never be the same again.

I pondered: I have gifts to share.
I too, can give. I laughed a long slow laugh;
my body eased, the anguished years melted in my memory
and Tabitha, looking up, laughed with me.

Think about these things...
A Widow of Joppa

Have you known a good friend on whom you depended? Then she moved away or got interested in someone else. How did you cope with the loss? Did you find another friend? Did you reach outside youself and grow stronger and more able to cope with change?

A Glimpse of... Rhoda

This story occurs during a time of persecution of the early church. James, the son of Zebedee, has been beheaded at Herod's order. Now Peter resides in Antonia prison waiting execution. Four guards prevent escape, chains bind him as well. Peter sleeps peacefully until he is awakened by an angel who slips him out of his bonds and delivers him to the street. Being barely awake, Peter believes this to be a dream, until he stands in the city street and the angel leaves him. Peter heads quickly for Mary's house.

In the courtyard Rhoda, a servant in the house, waits sleepily. Mary's house may have been the site of the Last Supper and became the headquarters of the new church. Rhoda's reaction to Peter's knocking demonstrate a curious, though very human attitude. She flies inside to share the news, without letting Peter in.

PRAYER: God, we thank you that you love us, even when we are impetuous and heedless. Give us the certainty that Rhoda possessed, so we may speak for you. Amen.

Rhoda

Acts 12:12-17

In Mary's house they met
a solemn group,
meeting to pray to God
for Peter's safe release.

Herod had captured Peter
through he had committed no offense,
save his preaching that the man called Jesus
had conquered death and risen to his God.

I was the doorkeeper
of the outer door in the courtyard.
By now it was midnight.
The group gathered before dark
and I only wanted to be given leave
to go to bed and sleep until the dawn.

A knock upon the gate!
My eyes flew open.
Who was knocking at this time of night?
I crept up to the gate
"Who is there?" I whispered.
"Peter," came the reply.
Peter!

I could not wait to tell the group inside.
I flew to share the news.

They were deep in prayer,
but I must interrupt them.

"Peter," I blurted out, "is at our gate."
They sat like stones.
"You're out of your mind, girl," one said.
"No," I insisted. "He's there knocking now."
"It's his angel," they countered.
(This was the day that Peter was to die.)

A Glimpse of Biblical Women & Other Poems

The room grew quiet. Then they heard the knocking.
A small group led the way across the courtyard.

Peter must have heard the shuffle of their feet.
He stopped knocking.
"Who is it?" one whispered.
"Peter," came the reply.

The bolt slid noiselessly back
the gate opened.
Peter, unharmed, stood in our courtyard.

Miracle!

Think about these things...
Rhoda

Rhoda is the impetuous but well meaning servant. The disciples gathered in Mary's house do not believe in miracles.

Have you ever been certain that something was true, only to be disbelieved by your friends? Has your impetuousity ever gotten you into trouble?

Can you imagine the surprise and relief with which Peter's friends enfolded him and took him into their house?

Other Poems

Preface to Other Poems

In these twenty-eight additional poems Dorothy Mosher turns from the evocation of Biblical women to poems covering a wide range of topics—prayers for the times of a day ("May My First Waking Thought," "Evening Prayer") or of a year ("Leaf Time in Pennsylvania," "April's Brief Affair with Winter") or of a life ("The Retirement Window," "All of Your Life is One with God"). Several poems are prayers for God's presence in the daily activities of life ("Prayer While Making Communion Bread," "Invitation"). Some are narrative poems, reflecting a trip to the British Isles:("A Sense of Place," "An English Idyll") or the moving of a loved object to a different place ("The Creche in the Kitchen"). Some are prayers for wisdom in discerning and doing God's will, references to Celtic spirituality, a poet's acknowledgement of sometime-faltering gifts. In all, a rich collection. Many are in metered unrhymed verse, others are skillfully rhymed. All are worthy of a reader's reflective attention. Two poems, on repeated readings of the whole group, stand out for me. "First Lent" is a haunting, dramatic portrayal of Jesus at the close of his forty days in the wilderness when
"His purpose set,
   His thoughts turned toward the Gallilee."
and then this beautiful concluding image:

"In a rocky hollow
  that his sandals touched
  a desert flower
  opened carmine petals
       to the sun."

The second of the poems that seemed to call my name was a much less dramatic poem, "Getting Through the Days," in which the believer waits and waits for God's presence and is visited by a simple revelation. I won't tell you what it is.. Read the poem!
I have known this writer for several years. I am grateful to her and I commend her for this work of her pen (or her computer), of her mind and heart and soul.
                    Martha Whitmore Hickman

May My First Waking Thought...

May my first waking thought

be of you, O God.

Sliding from sleep to consciousness.

In that silken moment

with the minds' voices mute,

may you shine in transcendent beauty

within the thousand altars of my soul.

Flood my heart and mind

with your presence

so I may glide from bed

singing alleleuias.

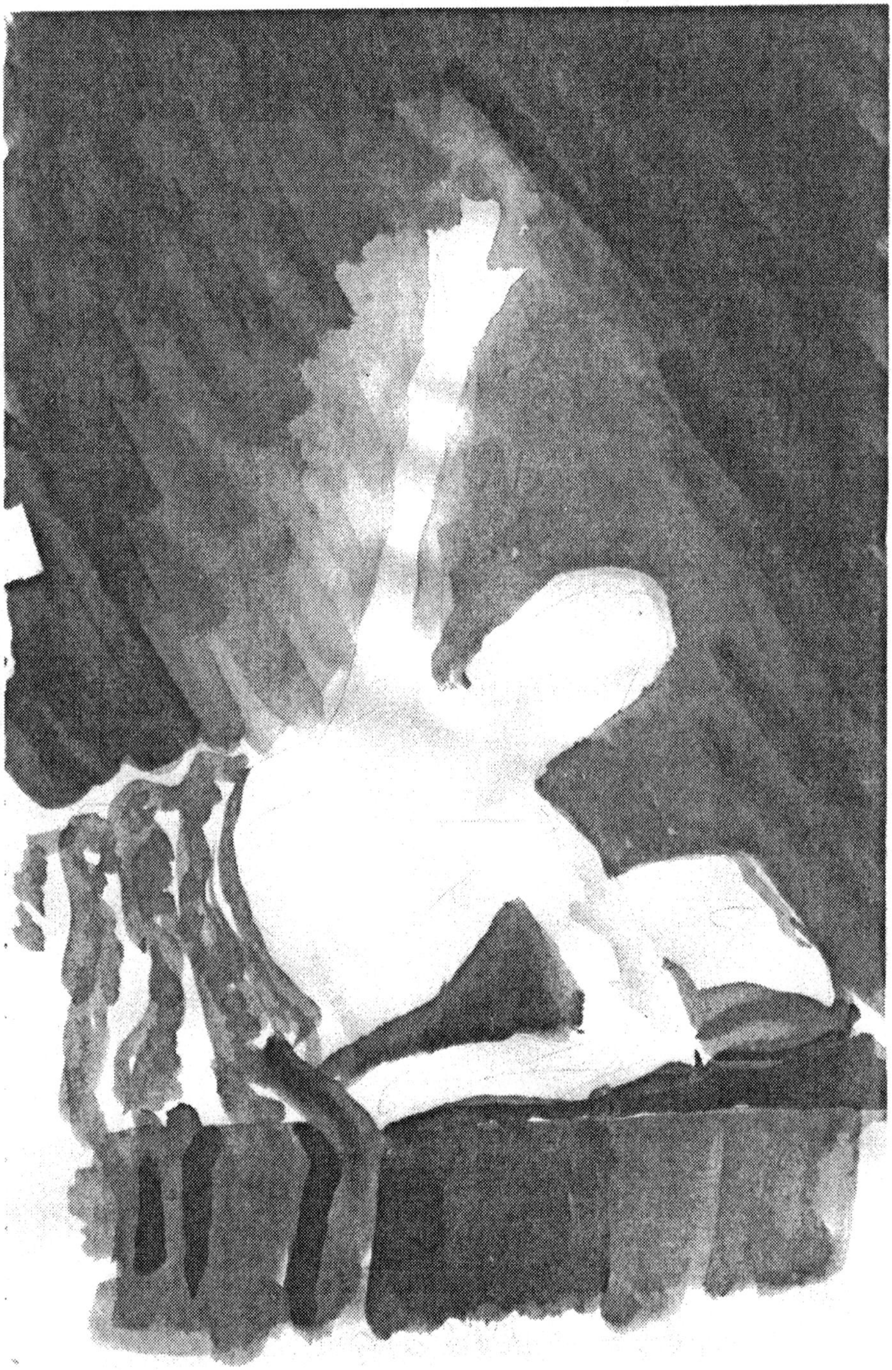

Evening Prayer

May I lie down this night

with mind wiped clean of care;

no looming trace of fear,

no waiting worries scare.

May my last waking thought,

Oh, keeper of my soul,

be of you. May I rest

secure in your control.

Bread

Even as dough rising in the pan

needs a warm comfortable place

to fulfill its mission and become bread,

so I feel the warmth of your presence,

Oh God. Help me be tender

and flavor my actions with your love.

May I be as bread to someone I meet this day.

All of Your Life Is One with God

All of your life is one with God

At birth - a shrill cry,

The zest for life in childhood,

The fancied dreams of youth.

God is with you in your holy days

And in your days of passion.

As you toil God's veiled hand guides you

And when you die, God's gracious arms enfold you.

All of your life is one with God.

A Glimpse of Biblical Women & Other Poems

First Lent

He looked so like his cousin, John
the lone spare figure:
gaunt faced, hollow eyed,
emerging from the desert wilderness
after forty days of fasting/prayer
to sink upon a stone.

Starving - his parched throat so dry
he could not even speak,
He stared in stupor over shifting sands;
then shielded his eyes,
in disbelieving wonder.

Angels - ministering angels - winging low
flew toward him.
Numbly he waited.

With blessed rush of wings the angels came
they offered bread and wine.
He wolfed the bread,
gulped wine,
wolfed bread again.

The demons, never far away
shielded their eyes for fear
of being blinded by angelic light.
They kicked up dust whorls to obscure his view.
He smiled, as one would smile at children's play.

Now stomach full, thirst slaked,
He stretched and smiled again.
New energy seeped into heart and lungs.
He stood - his head now clear.
His purpose set,
His thoughts turned toward the Galilee.

In a rocky hollow
that his sandals touched
a desert flower
opened carmine petals
to the sun.

Getting Through The Days

We cut the cord of continuity
severed past connections
cast ourselves loose
  to wait...
the wait grew long
we murmured dissent
tried to fill our days
with harmless, aimless tasks.

Advent was waiting time.
We waited for a word to set us free
but none came.
Now Lent has come
and we are waiting still.

What do we do to make our days
  have meaning?
I think I know the answer:
PRACTICING THE PRESENCE OF GOD
as Celtic Christians have
throughout the ages.
Forgetting the waiting
Each day is too short
to do the work God needs done in God's name.

Invitation

Come, Lord, I light the fire

—logs laid with care—

I sweep the floor and lintel

clean. The warm bare

wood of the table glows

with lustrous shine,

mirroring flames,

while I refine

words that speak my yearning.

"Oh, searcher of my soul,

I hide no more.

Come with your spirit, cleanse me

as you have before.

I wait to talk with you

in sheer delight.

Banished all other gods

or idols bright

all icons overturning."

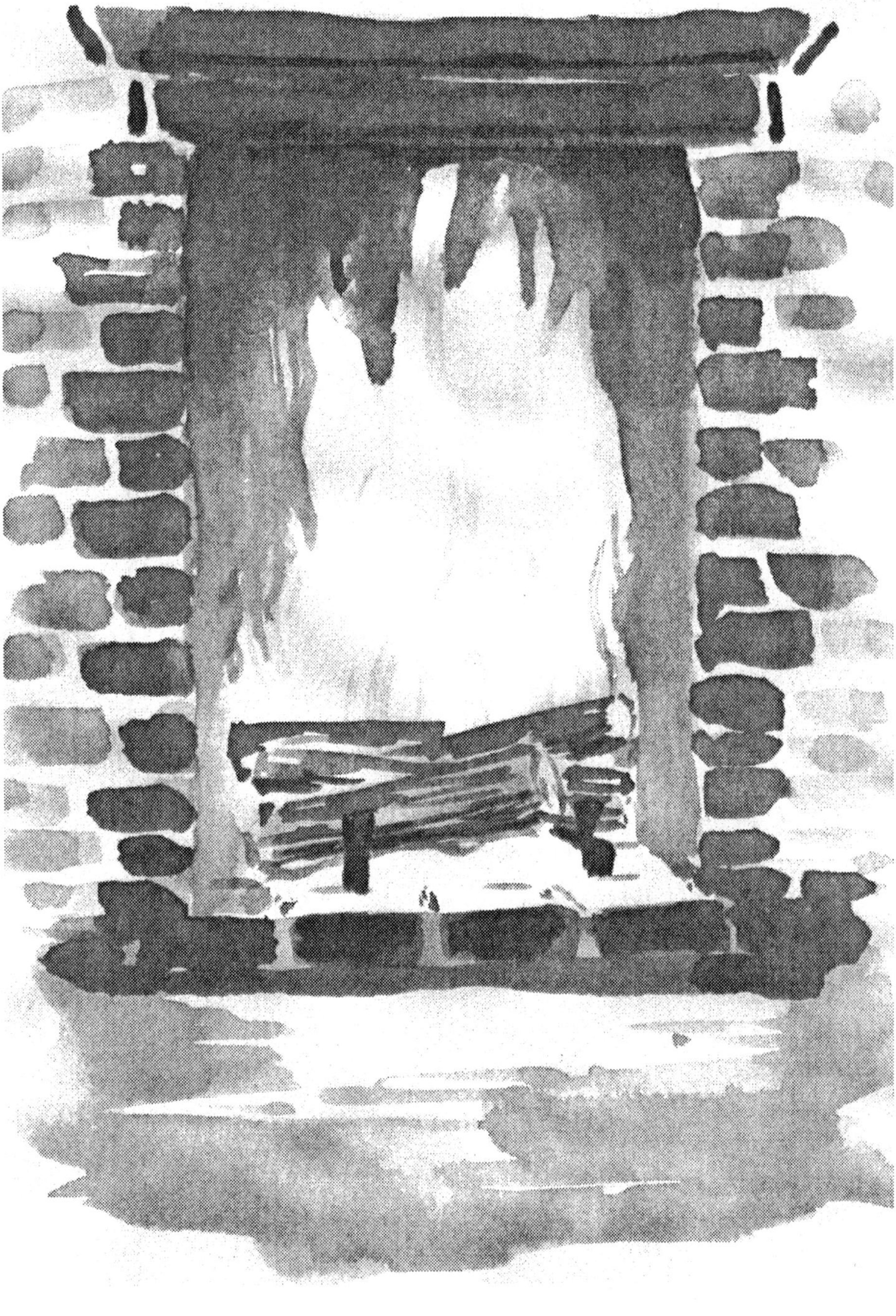

The Creche In The Kitchen

Tradition placed our creche in window seat.
The children loved to play the story
Setting up the shepherds, wise men,
angel, radiating glory.

Italian molded plaster figures
purchased wisely years before
told the story in their persons
"Come and worship. Come - Adore."

New this year our creche location
Set on kitchen table low.
Light from candle softly glimmers
light from shelf above aglow.

―――――

The way the light fell over Jesus' face,
illumined Mary, Joseph in their gratitude
made creche become a sudden sacred space
and our tradition altered by beatitude.

Leaf Time in Pennsylvania

We hold our breath in speechlessness
at royal palette grandly spread.
Bright sun illuminates the leaves
in seven shades of red.

The lowest brach, the highest tree
flaunts colors only Fall achieves.
An oak wears on its outer limbs
a gaudy scarf of claret leaves.

When soon this gracious scene is gone
and Winter's bite devours the land.
This view's enough to warm the heart
till Spring shall Winter's grip remand.

Crossroads

Conference Point Camp, Wisconsin

Our paths joined
at CROSSROADS
trails of our lives
coming together

paths of pain...
  and joy...
paths of uncertainty...

There is no path
that leads directly
to the Kingdom of God.
We search, we stumble,
we fall, we pick ourselves up
knowing that being on the path
to the Kingdom
is as much as we are allowed
and sometimes, more than we deserve.

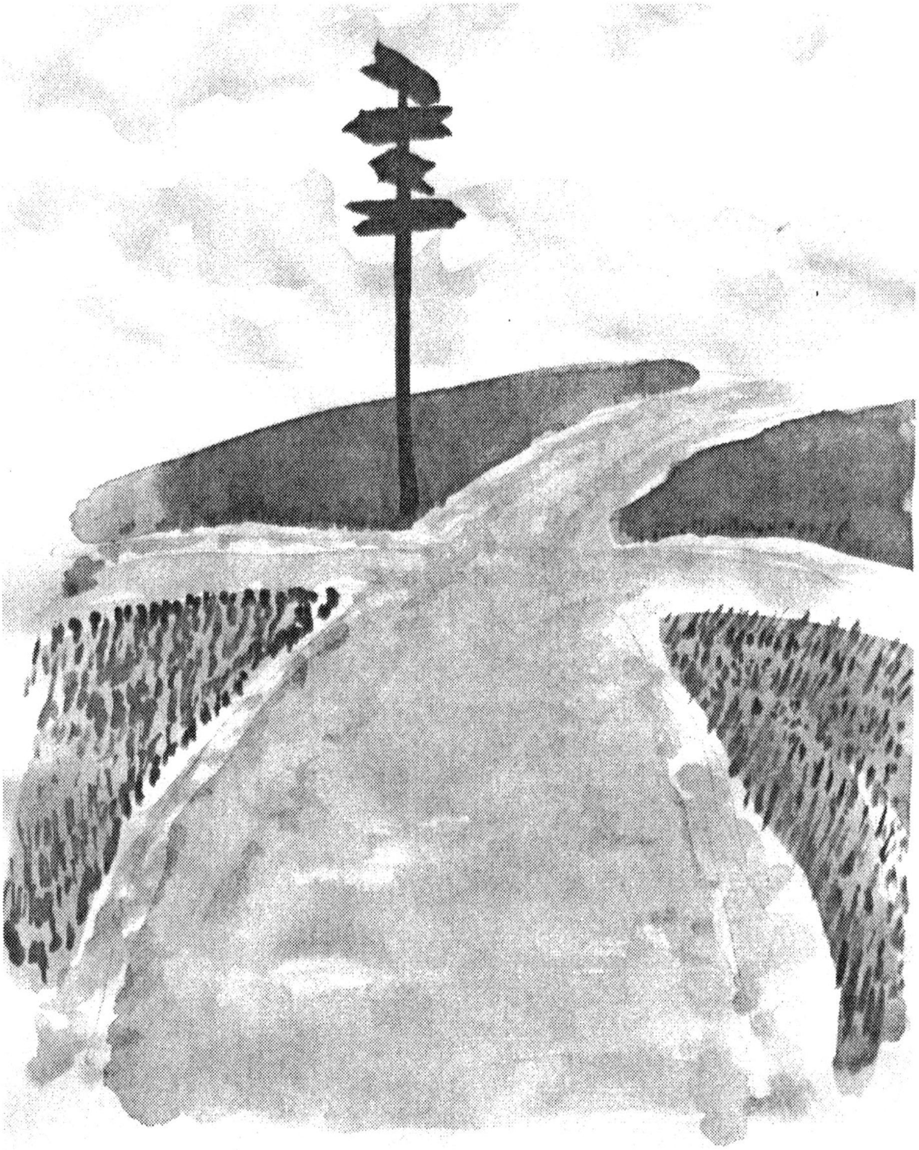

Prayer While Making Communion Bread

Be as yeast to me, O God
that I may carry your word to others.

Be as water to me
to smooth out the cares of living.

Be as flour to me
to give shape to my dreams and goals.

Be as oil that I may be peaceable.

Be as salt to give my life zest.

I am a child of yours.

Make me good bread to share with the world.

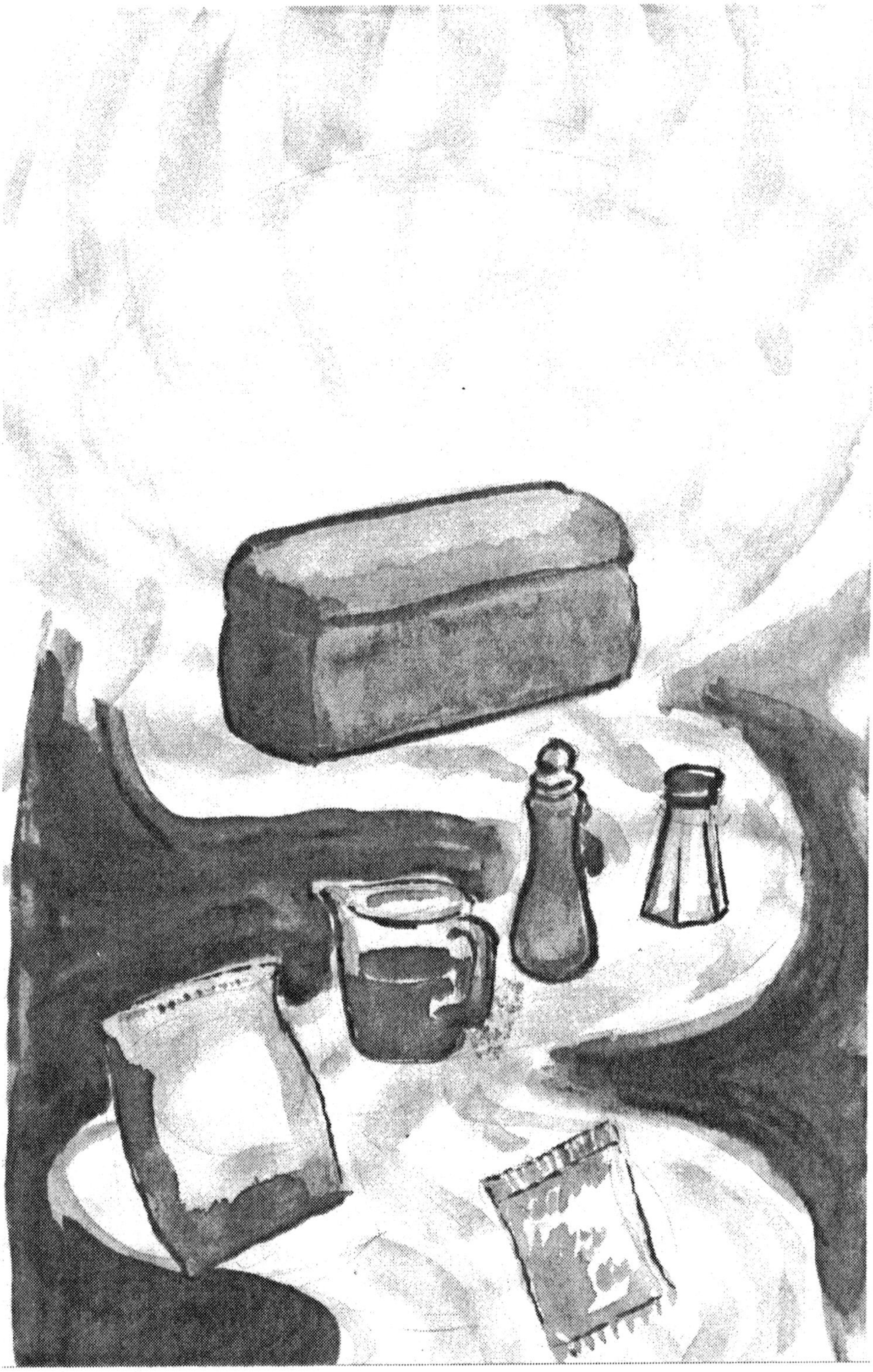

An English Idyll

Rain in the morning
rain in the evening
but in between — a perfect day.

Russell Square Underground
packed with humanity
London has inhabitants from
 all around the world
(England colonized these countries
and their people are colonizing Britain.)

Elevator down to the rails
Picadilly Line (Royal Blue)
to Earl's Court,
change to the District Line (Green)
for the journey to Kew.

This is a trip of remembrance.
Our first day in London
We hiked from Richmond to Kew.
(A titled picture of the Pagoda
rests within our photo album.)
This day will be our last in England.

We walk toward the gates of the Royal
 Botanical Gardens.
We buy our senior tickets
and walk into the shiny modern building
with a gift shop and snack bar,
both built since we last visited.
Then out into the park and its miles of road
We walk and remember the other times at Kew.

In a secluded part of the park
we find the Pavillion Restaurant.
Our hunger drives us inside.

Bruce buys a bowl of chili,
I buy a scone with toppings.
We both buy milk.

Outside under the grape arbor
clusters of chairs and tables await the diners.
Sun dapples the grape vines.
A stray vine falls on Bruce noiselessly.
He tucks it into the vines above.

I open my scone, spread clotted cream
   from Cornwall, thickly,
top with strawberry jam,
and take my first bite.

There may be better days or better places,
but I don't want to know them.
Eden for an hour here
is quite sufficient.

Pantry

Jesus, I'm here at the pantry again.
The piles of snack cookies, canned peas
and pineapple block my view.

I shudder at the disarray:
dusty dishes crammed into a box,
an old tea kettle, piles of shoes, a lamp.
I, who pride myself on a tidy house
come to work each week
in this humbling place.

Jesus, how must it feel
never to know that smell of new bought clothes,
to live with others' hand-me-downs -
discarded clothes someone no longer needs.

Jesus, help me heed you
in all the faces I will see today,
for you are surely here...
wearing an old coat,
with run-down shoes - and hungry.

A Glimpse of Biblical Women & Other Poems

Celtic Prayer for a Garden

Oh God, who created all the lovely plants that grow
and gave them to us for daily food,
we thank you for this wee strip of land
beside our fence, with plenty of sun
and earth we have enriched with peat and compost.

We asked you to bless the wee carrots
that came up when we thought the ground was barren.
We will enjoy their crispness with a cheese dip.

You blessed the tomatoes who bore fruit
from June until October,
so we could share with neighbors
and also make tomato sauce.

And also blessed the lettuce
so green and fruitful
that we could pick for sandwiches
and for our evening salad.

You blessed the beans which bloomed and set
pods, so we were able to supplement our meals
around their green goodness.

And for the onions, which disappointed us,
we ask to be given better judgement in planting
next year, so they do not hide under bean leaves.

Now it is Autumn
and the garden is empty,
but we can see it in our mind's eye
as we hope to make a better Eden next year.

All praise to you, God, the Master Gardener.

All praise to you, Christ Jesus
who loved to eat with sinners.

All praise to you, Holy Spirit.
Blow gently o'er your land
and make it fruitful next year.
      Amen

Daily Obligation

Daily I build my cairn of faith
course on course I build:

Bedrock of spiritual discipline
adoration's polished gemstone
pebble of silence
serrated blue slate of confession
banded rock of Bible study
layered shale of intercession.

All these combine
to build a shrine
of holy stones
to worship you, O God.

April's Brief Affair with Winter

April's brief affair with winter
—more flirtation than embrace
showered limbs and lawns with layers
of frigid lace.

Forsythia caught half a-leafing
topped by puffs of clinging snow.
Snowflake kamikazes bombing
streets and cars below.

Soon the sun beamed benediction
on that most unlikely pair,
but when April turned to kiss him,
Winter wasn't there.

Illumined

Candle flame leaps

-heroic paladin -

its golden tongue

sinks below candle's rim:

candle's yellow glow

flickering from within.

Lord, may your holy light

shine and discipline

my spirit, till I trust

you, my origin;

till adoration glows

illumined from within.

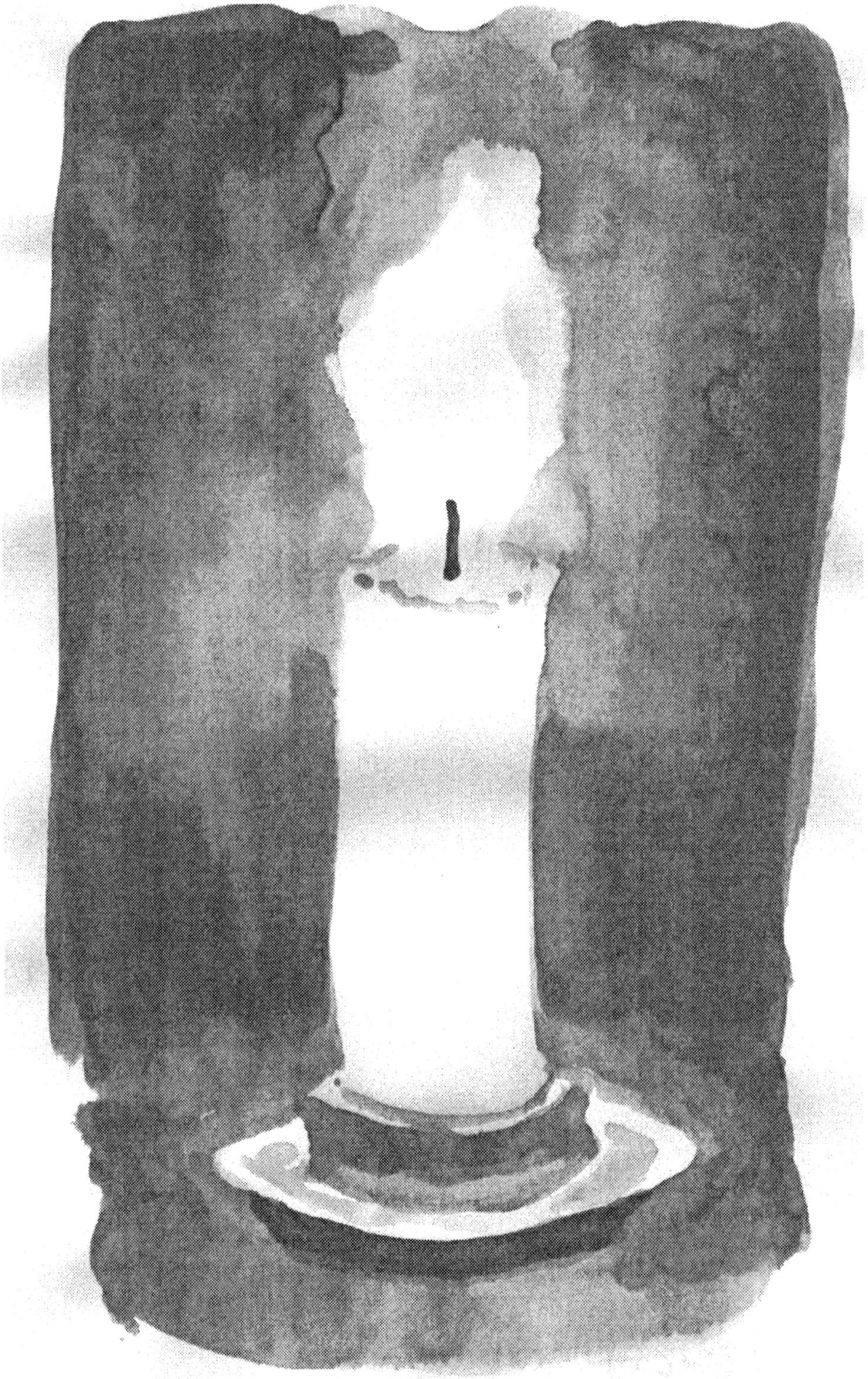

Smooring the Fire

Celtic woman smoored the fire:
embers spread upon the slate,
made a circle in three parts,
prayed a prayer to consecrate,

Prayed to God, to Christ and Spirit,
Thanks for covered warmth and light.
Fire: both miracle and friend
smothered in the ash at night.

In the morning before dawn
she bends down and adds new peat
fire blazes red and warm
filling room with light and heat.

Thus each morning she renews
precious fire from sleeping coals.
May the embers of our faith
fan the fires in our souls.

I Will Write My Poems...

I will write my poems this spring
but when I've finished them
I will hide them away
  out of sight
like people used to do with Mongol children.

Poor poems!
You limp and drool!
You do not sing,
Yet, you are the only songs
I write this spring.

Ever Widening Circles

Tune: Hymn to Joy

God, you ordered all creation, blew your breath into our frame
Planted seeds of awe within us; called us to revere your name:
Bless our service that, like ripples from a pebble shall expand
Forming ever widening circles, as we follow your command.

Your creation honors circles: planet, star and galaxy,
Hoops and balls, the toys of children; rings that speak fidelity;
Singing circles by a campfire, groups where women learn and preach;
Wider spread the circles, wider; *agapé*, within our reach.

Keep us searching wider circles as your children we become,
Help us in your path to follow; your love our curriculum:
Joining hands as equal partners with all outcasts of the earth
Till we come to to know your goodness; till we come to know our worth.

A Glimpse of Biblical Women & Other Poems

Quiet Time

Light the sacred flame.
self-concern abate
center on God's name
let God's will dictate.

Kairos time begin:
blest reflection space.
sin kept deep within
bared to light and grace.

In confession plead
dross and sin remove.
strength and courage need
paired with work and love.

Snuff the candle out.
gone are fear and pain.
thankful and devout
Rise to life again.

Advice for Christians from C.S. Lewis

One [1]

If you cannot believe
God really cares for you,
Do not despair or grieve
or question what to do.
Just act as if you do,
and when your mind comes clear,
you'll find God's presence true,
strong, comforting and near.
If stumbling through your prayer
your words resemble stone,
Just act as if God's there.
You cannot pray alone.

Two [2]

If love of God is dulled and feelings do not come,
don't manufacture them, or make your heart numb.
Just ask yourself instead, "If I love God for sure
What would I do to show God my love was free and pure?"
And when you've answered that, go do it with all might,
and in that action learn God's length
      and breadth and height.[3]

[1] Paraphrased from *Mere Christianity* by C.S. Lewis
[2] IBID
[3] Ephesians 3:18

Thoughts From Study of 1 John

Walking the tightrope:
tension between striving
to be a Christian
while discerning one's worldliness.

Some who seek comfort
do not struggle.
They settle for what society
   selects as proper.
Some are frightened
   become rigid — seek control.

The trick is to keep the tension
between being worldly and Christian.
Steady — don't look down.
Walk surefooted across the abyss
keeping your eyes on Jesus.

A Sense of Place 1986

Some years ago I read a vital book

expounding values of a sense of place:

some plot of land, a house, a town, a brook,

that gave the author confidence and grace.

For one who'd moved my home as much as I

the choices seemed too numerous to name:

— the ordinary places and the high —

yet none of them struck chords within my frame.

Perhaps the place and I caught not a link.

Perhaps it lay ahead for me to find.

Some stirrings of a need pushed me to think

of peaceful places: beautiful, tree-lined.

Then this year, dream and purpose became one.

I saw Iona shining in the sun.

Snorkelers Need Not Apply

No more wading along the biblical shoals

Let me dive into eras of pre-history

Swim in a sea of song and story

examine the lagoons of language

paddle past the grottoes of myth and mystery

till I surface....

clearing my head from the exigetical bends.

The Retirement Window

I watch the seasons change
behind my window square:
the sudden greens of spring,
the tulip bulbs aflare.

The lambent light of June
sifts through the maple's leaves,
an enterprising squirrel
leaps from his wire trapeze.

I watch the leaves float down,
the goldens and the reds,
trees stripped to basic shapes,
leaves safe in compost beds.

So from my window square
I watch each season's gift
with thankful eyes that see
year's passage - sweet and swift.

Relationships

(For Annie)

Relationships take two who are committed
to learning from each other over time,
tracing memories and life experience
having fun, and singing crazy rhyme.

Relationships do not emerge as full blown,
but as pieces of a puzzle, as souls bared,
requiring empathy and comprehension
of joys and sadness in the lives we've shared.

Relationships through time grow more than precious
for *kairos*, rules our talks, no *chronos*, here.
as if we'd only just before been talking
instead of only once or twice a year.

Relationships take years to verify,
but it is less than human not to try.

Thanks Times Five

A patient in a mental hospital
in deep depression, found his way
after counsel, when he thought of
five reasons for his thanks each day.

If during quiet time I try to tread
that path of thankfulness with five
small happenings that bless my day,
I find my spirit comes alive.

And if my mind's too jumbled, self-contained
to find five reasons for my gratitude,
I need to spend more time with God
in centered prayer and quiet mood.

Oh God, just five good reasons why
I'm thankful may seem picayune
yet, that can be the remedy
to help my soul attune.

Printed in the United States
31938LVS00003B/181-213